BREAK THE LANGUAGE BARRIER LEVEL 1
vickimariechats@gmail.com

INTRODUCTION

This is a book that will help you to speak and understand Spanish. It has been designed to help you communicate effectively on a day-to-day basis. It will encourage you to take the building blocks of the Spanish language and construct your own phrases, questions, and conversations. It is not holiday Spanish, nor is it Phrasebook Spanish. Neither will it blind you with grammatical science, but rather will present both English and Spanish Grammar in the most simplistic way possible.

I have developed this method, and I have been exactly where you are now. Over more than 20 years of teaching Spanish to Expats in Spain I believe I have developed the most simplistic method possible to help people come to grips with what is often a confusing and bewildering language, but also a beautiful one that can enrich your life in many ways.

This book is not intended solely as a substitute for classes, which really are the best way to learn, but rather as a complement or a supplement to them. However, I am aware that many of you either do not have time for classes or feel uncomfortable in a classroom situation, so this course is the next best thing. It is backed up with You Tube tutorials to practice pronunciation.

Learning a new language is not an overnight thing, it takes time and patience, but the key is to enjoy it and not take it too seriously. Relax, enjoy it, be kind to yourself and accept that mistakes are part of the learning process. Do not be afraid to "have a go" at speaking Spanish, even though you will say things wrong, communication is the key. If you make yourself understood, it does not matter if you do not say every single word correctly, only the most important ones!! Always focus on what you have learned, not what you still do not know, and accept that perfection is perhaps too high a goal to set for yourself in the beginning.

Most of all, I hope you enjoy it and find, as I have, the pure pleasure in learning a beautiful language such as Spanish, which is spoken so widely across the world. You will, along the way, learn much about your own language also. On the completion of this book accompanied by the YouTube tutorials, you should be confident enough to have a basic conversation in the present tense in Spanish, and be ready to move on to Level 2.

Te deseo éxito.
Vicki

BREAK THE LANGUAGE BARRIER LEVEL 1
vickimariechats@gmail.com

INDEX

		Page Number
1.	ALPHABET AND PRONUNCIATION	3
2.	MASCULINE AND FEMININE	9
3.	NUMBERS	10
4.	NUMBERS PRACTICE	11
5.	CLOTHES AND NUMBERS	12
6.	¿QUE HORA ES? - WHAT TIME IS IT?	12
7.	PRACTICA LA HORA	16
8.	THE FIRST VERB "TO BE" - "SER"	18
9.	DESCRIPTIONS SER - MASCULINE AND FEMININE ADJECTIVES	20
10.	THE VERB "SER" IN CONTEXT	21
11.	CONVERSATION PRACTICE "SER"	23
12.	THE SECOND VERB "TO BE" - "ESTAR"	24
13.	DESCRIPTIONS- "ESTAR"	26
14.	"ESTAR" IN CONTEXT	27
15.	TRANSLATION "ESTAR"	29
16.	CONVERSATION PRACTICE- "ESTAR"	30
17.	COPPPRINCT/ FLOMMETS	31
18.	CONVERSATION PRACTICE "SER" V "ESTAR"	32
19.	"HAY"	33
20.	"HAY"/ "ESTAR"/ "SER"	34
21.	DESCRIBING PEOPLE	36
22.	¿QUIEN ES? / ¿QUIENES SON?	37
23.	LA CASA DE PEDRO	40
24.	REGULAR VERBS - 1ST CONJUGATION - 'AR' VERBS	42
25.	"AR" VERBS IN CONTEXT	49
26.	2ND CONJUGATION - "ER" VERBS	52
27.	"ER" VERBS IN CONTEXT	56
28.	3RD CONJUGATION - 'IR' VERBS	59
29.	TRANSLATION FROM ENGLISH TO SPANISH - REGULAR VERBS	62
30.	ADVERBS OF FREQUENCY	63
31.	CONVERSATION PRACTICE OF REGULAR VERBS	64
32.	PRACTICE OF REGULAR VERBS	65
33.	DIPHTHONGS - ROOT OR STEM CHANGING VERBS	67
34.	DIPHTHONGS - CONVERSATION PRACTICE	73
35.	DIPHTHONGS IN CONTEXT	74
36.	THE VERB "TENER" - TO HAVE	76
37.	"GO-GO" VERBS	79
38.	"GUSTAR"	80
39.	"TO GO" - THE HIGHLY IRREGULAR 'IR' VERB	82
40.	AUNT CARMEN/ TIA CARMEN	83
41.	POSTSCRIPT	86
42.	KEY TO "TOP TIPS"	87
43.	ANSWERS	88

Copyright© Vicki Marie Riley 1999-2026. All rights reserved.

1. ALPHABET AND PRONUNCIATION

The Alphabet

The Spanish alphabet is pronounced completely differently to the English one and as you see below it has two extra letters.

PRACTICE A: Listen to the YouTube video 1 and practice the pronunciation, noticing the difference especially in the vowel sounds.

A ah	N eh-ne
B beh	Ñ en-yeh
C the	O oh
D deh	P peh
E eh	Q coo
F eh-fe	R eh-reh
G he	S es-seh
H ah-che	T teh
I ee	U oo
J hota	V oo-beh
K ka	W oo-beh doh-ble
L eh-le	X eh-kiss
Ll el-yeh	Y ee-gree-eh-ga
M eh-meh	Z the-ta

Pronunciation rules

-Words ending in a **vowel**, or the letters "n" or "s" are stressed on the next to last syllable - e.g. bo**te**lla, **ham**bre, **jer**sey.
-Words ending in another consonant take the stress on the last syllable - e.g. pa**pel**, re**loj**, mu**jer**, Mad**rid**.
-Exceptions are indicated by a written accent - e.g. **lám**para, televi**sión**, **mú**sica.

BREAK THE LANGUAGE BARRIER LEVEL 1
vickimariechats@gmail.com

PRACTICE B: Find the meaning of these words in your dictionary and practice saying them

A- "ah"
adiós
anoche
antes
avión

B - "beh":
botella
banco
balón

C-"theh"

"theh" ("c" plus "i" or "e")	"k" ("c" plus "a" ,"o" or "u")	"qw"
cerdo	carta	cuando
cine	como	cuatro
gracias	cubo	cuerpo

D- "deh"
delfín
dentro
deporte

E-"eh"
elefante
edad
elegante
-

F- "effeh"
falda
falso
fecha

G-"he "heh"

(g plus e)	"hee"(g plus i)	"ga" (g plus a)	"go" (g plus o)
coger	gimnasio	gasolina	golf
general	girasol	gato	gol
gente	girar	gastar	gota

H- "ah-che-Always silent
hospital
hotel
ahora

I- "ee"
iglesia
inglés
imposible

J- "hota"
ojo
caja
jugar

K- "ka"
kilo
kiosco
kárate

L- "eleh"
los
local
luna

LL- "elyeh"
llamar
llave
paella

M- "emeh"
más
martes
mesa

N- "eneh"
negro
nata
nada

Ñ- "enyeh"
niño
mañana
año

P- "peh"
pan
palo
pago

Q- "coo"
queso
que
querer

R- "erre"
recibo
red
regalo

S- "esse"
saludo
salsa
sal

T- "teh"
tabaco
tarde
teclado

U- "oo"
uno
urgente
uso

V- "oo-beh"
vaca
vale
uva

W- "oo-beh-doh-ble"
web
windsurf
walkman

X- "eh-kiss"

Xilófono

Extra

Y- "ee-gree-eh-ga"

yate

yeso

yo

Z- "theta"

zapatos

luz

pez

 Top Tips!!

1. Grammatical terms:

Nouns- Naming words -E.g. House, car, book, man, woman, cup etc.
Adjectives- Describing words - E.g. Nice, cold, big, small, red, blue, tall, pretty.
Verbs- Doing words- E.g. To drink, to laugh, to eat, to sleep, to be, to speak, to write.
Prepositions- Joining words- E.g. with, to, at etc.

2. Adjectives:

Adjectives (describing words) generally follow the noun (naming word) in Spanish unlike English where they precede it.
E.g. Es un coche grande- It is a big car.
      Es una mujer bonita- She is a pretty woman.

Colours are also adjectives and follow the same rule.
E.g. El coche negro-The black car.
      La casa blanca- The white house.

Note also that they must correspond to masculine or feminine also, and singular or plural. They also require an "s" or "es" for plural. Add "s" for adjectives ending in a vowel, and "es" for those ending in a consonant.

PRACTICE SPELLING YOUR NAME

¿Cómo te llamas? What´s your name?

Me llamo ....

I am called ....

¿Cómo se escribe? How do you spell it?

....

¿Y de apellido? And your surname?

Mi apellido es ....

¿Cómo se escribe? How do you spell it?

....

2. MASCULINE AND FEMININE

A noun is a 'naming' word. Any word that tells us the name of something is a noun-car, table, man, telephone etc. In Spanish, all nouns have a gender, that is they are masculine or feminine.

Generally, any noun that ends in 'a' such as botella (bottle), casa (house) or chica (girl), would be feminine. However, there are exceptions such as agua (water) and problema (problem) which are masculine.

Because of this distinction, there are different ways of saying 'the' (definite article) and "a/an/some" (indefinite articles) in Spanish, depending on whether the noun is masculine or feminine.

E.g. the book - el libro a book - un libro -the house - la casa a house - una casa

PRACTICE A: Find the Spanish word for the following in your dictionary and decide whether or not they should be "el" or "la", "un" or "una".

1. The office
2. A doctor
3. The car
4. A skirt
5. The airport
6. A teacher
7. The dog
8. A star
9. The train
10. A supermarket
11. The computer
12. A magazine
13. The restaurant
14. A chair

Masculine plural and feminine plural.

E.g. the books - los libros some books - unos libros

the houses - las casas some houses - unas casas

PRACTICE B: Translate the following, remembering that we add 'es' to nouns ending in a consonant.

1. The flowers
2. Some potatoes
3. The drinks
4. Some buildings
5. The banks
6. Some shops
7. The tables
8. Some newspapers.
9. The telephones
10. Some wardrobes
11. The kitchens
12. Some gardens

3. NUMBERS

PRACTICE A: Practice saying these numbers out loud

1	Uno	39	Treinta y nueve	77	Setenta y siete
2	Dos	40	Cuarenta	78	Setenta y ocho
3	Tres	41	Cuarenta y uno	79	Setenta y nueve
4	Cuatro	42	Cuarenta y dos	80	Ochenta
5	Cinco	43	Cuarenta y tres	81	Ochenta y uno
6	Seis	44	Cuarenta y cuatro	82	Ochenta y dos
7	Siete	45	Cuarenta y cinco	83	Ochenta y tres
8	Ocho	46	Cuarenta y seis	84	Ochenta y cuatro
9	Nueve	47	Cuarenta y siete	85	Ochenta y cinco
10	Diez	48	Cuarenta y ocho	86	Ochenta y seis
11	Once	49	Cuarenta y nueve	87	Ochenta y siete
12	Doce	50	Cincuenta	88	Ochenta y ocho
13	Trece	51	Cincuenta y uno	89	Ochenta y nueve
14	Catorce	52	Cincuenta y dos	90	Noventa
15	Quince	53	Cincuenta y tres	91	Noventa y uno
16	Dieciséis	54	Cincuenta y cuatro	92	Noventa y dos
17	Diecisiete	55	Cincuenta y cinco	93	Noventa y tres
18	Dieciocho	56	Cincuenta y seis	94	Noventa y cuatro
19	Diecinueve	57	Cincuenta y siete	95	Noventa y cinco
20	Veinte	58	Cincuenta y ocho	96	Noventa y seis
21	Veintiuno	59	Cincuenta y nueve	97	Noventa y siete
22	Veintidós	60	Sesenta	98	Noventa y ocho
23	Veintitrés	61	Sesenta y uno	99	Noventa y nueve
24	Veinticuatro	62	Sesenta y dos	100	Cien
25	Veinticinco	63	Sesenta y tres	101	Ciento uno
26	Veintiséis	64	Sesenta y cuatro	102	Ciento dos
27	Veintisiete	65	Sesenta y cinco	103	Ciento tres
28	Veintiocho	66	Sesenta y seis	104	Ciento cuatro (etc)
29	Veintinueve	67	Sesenta y siete	200	Doscientos
30	Treinta	68	Sesenta y ocho	300	Trescientos
31	Treinta y uno	69	Sesenta y nueve	400	Cuatrocientos
32	Treinta y dos	70	Setenta	500	Quinientos
33	Treinta y tres	71	Setenta y uno	600	Seiscientos
34	Treinta y cuatro	72	Setenta y dos	700	Setecientos
35	Treinta y cinco	73	Setenta y tres	800	Ochocientos
36	Treinta y seis	74	Setenta y cuatro	900	Novecientos
37	Treinta y siete	75	Setenta y cinco	1000	Mil
38	Treinta y ocho	76	Setenta y seis	1001	Mil uno (etc)

1,000,000 - Un millón

4. NUMBERS PRACTICE

Write out the following numbers in full.

1. 121
2. 567
3. 54
4. 1,457
5. 999
6. 632
7. 32
8. 768
9. 2,530
10. 5,324
11. 724
12. 17
13. 852
14. 15
15. 61
16. 333
17. 1,023
18. 155
19. 592
20. 431
21. 77
22. 888
23. 923
24. 67
25. 274
26. 92
27. 5,232
28. 24
29. 87
30. 165

5. CLOTHES AND NUMBERS

La Ropa – Clothes

Cost - Cuesta (singular) / Cuestan (plural)

1. Los guantes - gloves
2. La camisa – shirt
3. La bufanda – scarf
4. Los pantalones – trousers
5. Los zapatos – shoes
6. Los calcetines – socks
7. El jersey - jumper
8. La falda - skirt
9. La chaqueta - jacket
10. La camiseta – t-shirt
11. El vestido - dress
12. El sombrero - hat

Example questions and answers:

¿Cuánto cuesta la chaqueta? - How much does the jacket cost?

La chaqueta cuesta .... euros - The jacket costs ....

¿Cuánto cuestan los zapatos? - How much do the shoes cost?

Los zapatos cuestan .... euros - The shoes cost ....

PRACTICE A: Ask and answer questions about the clothes below.

1. 25.00 €
2. 31.99€
3. 9.99€
4. 15.44€
5. 18.70€
6. 9.99€
7. 33.60€
8. 47.20€
9. 45.20€
10. 33.62€
11. 90.00€
12. 18.71€

Top Tips!!

3. Punctuation tip:

In written Spanish, exclamations and questions are easily spotted as they begin with an inverted exclamation or question mark:
E.g. ¡Qué calor hace!- How hot it is!
¿Qué haces?- What are you doing?

4. Subject pronouns:

The subject prounouns I (yo), you (tú), he/she (él/ella), we (nosotros/as), you plural (vosotros/as) and they (ellos/ellas) are not normally necessary in Spanish. As the verb forms are usually unique, e.g "Soy" can only mean "I am", it is not necessary to say "yo soy". The subject pronouns are generally only used for emphasis, or where it is not clear which person it is, especially with he and she.

E.g. Ella está aquí- She is here.
Él está aquí- He is here.

5. Possesive adjectives:

My- mi/s
Your- tu/s
His/her-su/s
Our- nuestro/a/os/as
Your (plural)-vuestro/a/os/as
Their-su/s

Possesive adjectives have to agree in number and gender with the item/person we are describing, not the person who it belongs to.
E.g. Es nuestra casa- It is our house (house is feminine singular)
Son mis libros-They are my books (books are masculine plural)

6. ¿QUÉ HORA ES?

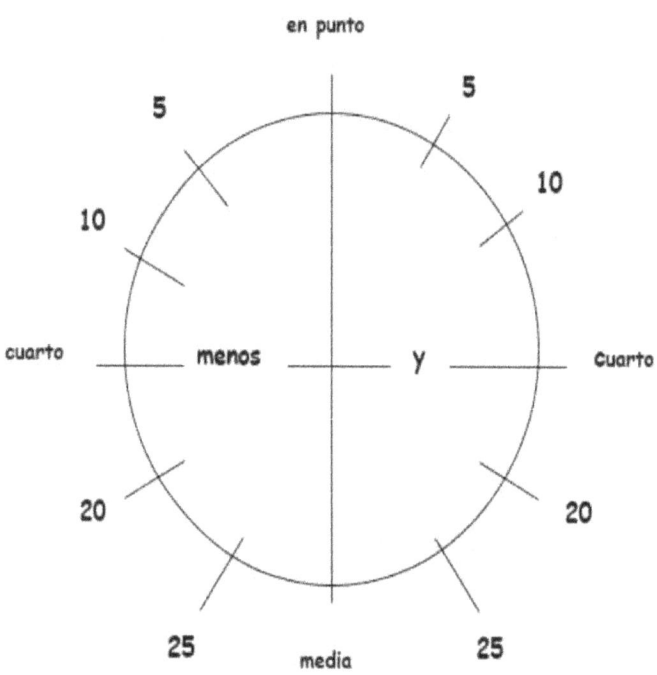

In Spanish, when we say "it is" for any time except 1 o'clock, we use "son las", e.g.

    a)   3 o'clock – **son las tres en punto**
    b)   4.30 – **son las cuatro y media/ son las cuatro y treinta**
    c)   9.45 – **son las diez menos cuarto/son las nueve y cuarenta y cinco/ son las diez menos quince.**

For any time using one o'clock, we use "es la", e.g.

    a) 1.15 – **es la una y cuarto/ es la una y quince**
    b) 12.55 – **es la una menos cinco/ son las doce y cincuenta y cinco**

Practice A: Write out the following times in full in Spanish.
Some can be said in more than one way. Write all of them.

1. It's 11.30

2. It's 3.45

3. It's 1.10

4. It's 12.35

5. It's 2 o'clock

6. It's 8.25

7. It's 9.20

8. It's 1.25

9. It's 10.30

10. It's 8.45

7. PRACTICA LA HORA

Salir : to leave   Llegar: to arrive   A: at

¿A qué hora sale el tren? -At what time does the train leave?

El tren sale a las doce.- The train leaves at 12.00.

¿A que hora llega el tren?- At what time does the train arrive?

El tren llega a las cuatro menos veinte. -The train arrives at 3.40.

PRACTICE A: Ask and answer as above using the information below.

		sale / llega
1.	El tren	10.15/8.00
2.	El autobús	11.10/5.30
3.	El avión	10.20/3.10
4.	El cartero	10.05/3.35
5.	El médico	8.45/9.45
6.	La enfermera	12.35/1.15
7.	La secretaria	4.45/2.30
8.	La señora	5.50/6.40
9.	La profesora	3.25/11.05
10.	Maria	1.20/6.25

PRACTICE B: Do the same using these different verbs.

C. Comenzar-To begin   Terminar-To finish

¿A qué hora <u>comienza</u> la pelicula? - At what time does the film start?

La pelicula <u>comienza</u> a las doce. - The film starts at 12.00.

¿A qué hora <u>termina</u> la pelicula? -At what time does the film finish?

La pelicula <u>termina</u> a las cuatro menos veinte. - The film finishes at 3.40.

		comienza/termina
1.	El partido	10.15/12.15
2.	El programa	4.15/5.30
3.	El espectaculo	10.20/3.10
4.	La feria	9.20/7.40
5.	El cantante	8.45/9.45
6.	La comida	1.30/3.50
7.	La fiesta	4.45/2.30
8.	La cena	10.10/1.15
9.	La clase	3.25/11.05
10.	El baile	11.30/4.00

8. THE FIRST VERB "TO BE" – "SER"

The verb "to be" can be complicated in Spanish as there are in fact 2 verbs that mean the same as in English, "ser" and "estar". So when we are speaking in Spanish we have to decide what we are saying we <u>are</u> so we can decide which one to use. Before we look at the verbs, it is a good idea to look at the verb in English first.

INFINITIVE	TO BE
1st person singular	I am
2nd person singular	You are
3rd person singular	He/she/it is
1st person plural	We are
2nd person plural	You (s) are
3rd person plural	They are

What we have done above is taken the verb "to be" and conjugated it, which basically means put it into the 6 different persons. Every time we conjugate a verb, we will follow this pattern so although it may seem scary at first it does get easier, honest!!

Let´s now take the 1st verb to be in Spanish, "ser", and conjugate it alongside the English –

PERSON	TO BE (INFINITIVE)	SER (INFINITIVE)
1st person singular	I am	(yo) soy
2nd person singular	You are	(tú) eres
3rd person singular	He/she/it is	(Él/ella) es
1st person plural	We are	(nosotros/as) somos
2nd person plural	You (s) are	(vosotros/as) sois
3rd person plural	They are	(ellos/as) son

"Ser" is often known as the "permanent" verb in that it is generally used to describe anything we "permanently" are.

"Ser" is used for identity, nationality/origin, profession, and 'permanent' descriptions. Profession is an exception to the "permanent" rule as obviously it can change, but ser is always used to describe it.

So, I might say:

(Yo) soy Vicki.
(Yo) soy profesora de español.
(Yo) soy inglesa.
(Yo) soy de Manchester.
(Yo) soy baja.

PRACTICE A: Work out what they mean and write one similar sentence for each but about yourself.

PRACTICE B: Translate the following sentences into Spanish using the appropriate form of the verb "ser" and looking up any words you don´t know in the dictionary.

1. We are English.
2. The table is square.
3. Are you a doctor?
4. Are you(s) teachers?
5. She is tall.
6. They are from Spain.
7. I am Juan.
8. He is a waiter.
9. I am from the United States.
10. You(s) are my friends.
11. He is handsome.
12. She is very interesting.
13. They are French from Paris.
14. You(s) are teachers.
15. Today is Tuesday.
16. My socks are white.
17. Who are you?
18. Jennifer Aniston is an actress.

Try to learn off by heart the "SER" verb.

(yo) soy
(tú) eres
(Él/ella) es
(nosotros/as) somos
(vosotros/as) sois
(ellos/as) son

9. DESCRIPTIONS - Masculine and Feminine Adjectives

As we have seen, all nouns in Spanish are masculine or feminine. As a consequence of this, adjectives, i.e. describing words, including colours take an ending appropriate to their gender, i.e. an 'o' for masculine and 'a' for feminine.

e.g. El chico es alt**o** La chica es alt**a**
     El coche es roj**o** La falda es roj**a**

Also, they have to become plural if they are describing a plural noun.

e.g. **Los** chicos son alt**os** **Las** chicas son alt**as**
     Los coches son roj**os** **Las** faldas son roj**as**

However, adjectives that don't end in o, for example: **grande** or **difícil** do not change for masculine and feminine, but do require an "**s**" or "**es**" for plural. Add "**s**" for nouns adjectives ending in a vowel, and "**es**" for those ending in a consonant.
E.g.   The houses are big   **Las** casas son grand**es**
        The bars are cheap   **Los** bar**es** son barat**os**

If the nouns described are a mixture of masculine and feminine the masculine takes precedence.
E.g. John and Jane are American - John y Jane son american**os.**

PRACTICE A: Translate the following sentences into Spanish.

1. Restaurants are very cheap in Spain.
2. Wine is very expensive in England.
3. The house is big.
4. Peter and Mary are English.
5. Carmen and María are Spanish.
6. They (masc.) are tall.
7. The car is small.
8. The lamp is white.
9. The skirt is too small.
10. The corridor is narrow.
11. The kitchen is wide.
12. Spanish is easy.
13. You are famous.
14. She is famous.
15. We are parents.

10. THE VERB "SER" IN CONTEXT

PRACTICE A: Practice saying this conversation out loud.

CLASE DE ESPAÑOL

Klaus: ¡Hola! Soy Klaus.
Janet: Yo soy Janet.
Klaus: Encantado. Yo soy alemán, de Múnich.
¿Y tú Janet? ¿De dónde eres?
Janet: Soy inglesa, de Londrés.
Klaus: ¿Son ellos también ingleses?
Janet: No, no son ingleses. Paulo es italiano, de Roma. Claudia es francesa, de Paris. Frank es americano, de Nueva York.
¿Quién es el profesor de español?
Klaus: Pedro Pérez es el profesor.
Janet: ¿Cómo es Pedro Pérez?
Klaus: Es alto, moreno y muy simpático.
Janet: ¿Es español o argentino?
Klaus: Es español, de Madrid.

PRACTICE B: Pick out all the examples of the verb "ser". There are 16 in total. Then translate the text into English.

PRACTICE C: Translate these questions into Spanish, then answer in Spanish.

1. Where is Klaus from?
2. Where is Janet from?
3. Is Paulo Italian?
4. Is Claudia German?
5. Where is Frank from?
6. Who is the teacher?
7. What is Pedro Pérez?
8. What is Pedro Pérez like?
9. Where is Pedro Pérez from?
10. Where are you from?

PRACTICE D: *Conversation translation. Using the previous conversation as a guide, translate this conversation into Spanish.*

JOHN : Hello, I am Johnn. Who are you?
MARÍA: I am María. Are you a Spanish student?
JOHN : No, I am not a Spanish student, I am a German student. And you?
MARÍA: I am a German student also.
JOHN : Where are you from?
MARÍA: I am Spanish, from Alicante. And you?
JOHN : I am English, from Manchester.
MARÍA: Who is the German teacher?
JOHN : Mrs Schmidt.
MARÍA: What is she like?
JOHN : She is short, blonde, and very nice.

PRACTICE E: *Now translate the following questions into Spanish and answer them in Spanish.*

1. Is John a Spanish student?
2. Is María a Spanish student?
3. Where is María from?
4. Where is John from?
5. Who is the German teacher?
6. What is Mrs Schmidt like?
7. Who is your Spanish teacher?
8. What is he or she like?
9. Where are you from?
10. What are you like?

11. CONVERSATION PRACTICE- "SER" ONLY

PRACTICE A: Translate these questions into Spanish and answer in Spanish.

1. Where are you from?

2. What is your car like?

3. Which day is it today?

4. What time is it?

5. When is your birthday?

6. What is your favourite food?

7. Who is your favourite actor?

8. What colour is your house?

9. Why is Spanish necessary?

10. When is the Spanish Class?

11. Who is your best friend?

12. What are you like?

11. THE SECOND VERB "TO BE" - "ESTAR"

We have looked at the first verb "to be" in Spanish, "ser" which is used to talk about identity, origin, nationality, "permanent" descriptions and professions. Now we will look at the second verb "to be", "estar".

Here is the conjugation of "estar" and the English equivalent.

PERSON	TO BE (INFINITIVE)	ESTAR (INFINITIVE)
1st person singular	I am	(yo) estoy
2nd person singular	You are	(tú) estás
3rd person singular	He/she/it is	(Él/ella) está
1st person plural	We are	(nosotros/as) estamos
2nd person plural	You (s) are	(vosotros/as) estáis
3rd person plural	They are	(ellos/as) están

"Estar" is often known as the "temporary" verb in that it is generally used to describe anything we "temporarily" are.

"Estar" is used to talk about how we are in the moment, not how we always are. So we use it to describe moods, emotions, the way we feel and "temporary" descriptions of people or things. However, for marital status, we use "estar".

Another important exception is **LOCATION**. Whether permanent or temporary, whenever we are talking about WHERE someone or something is in Spanish, we **ALWAYS ALWAYS** use "estar".

So remember, **LOCATION LOCATION LOCATION**

ALWAYS "estar".

I might say:

(Yo) no estoy casada.
(Yo) estoy cansada.
(Yo) estoy en España.
(Yo) estoy contenta.
(Yo) estoy en casa.

PRACTICE A: *Work out what they mean and write 5 similar sentences about yourself.*

PRACTICE B: *Translate the following sentences into Spanish using the appropriate form of the verb "estar" and looking up any words you don't know in the dictionary. Remember the same rules apply re masculine, feminine and plural adjectives as we looked at earlier using "ser".*

1. I am with my husband.
2. I am not with my husband.
3. We are tired.
4. You (s) are happy.
5. They are sad.
6. Pedro and Carmen are in Madrid.
7. I am sad because you are not here.
8. Why aren't you happy?
9. Is he married or single?
10. She is in class and he is in the office.
11. The dogs are in the garden.
12. We are angry.
13. The sky is grey.
14. Begoña is divorced.
15. The coffee is cold.
16. How are you?
17. How is your friend Miguel?
18. Where is the Police Station?
19. Where are the envelopes?
20. How are you(s)?
21. You are very anxious.
22. Maria is ill.
23. Juan is married.
24. The two children are in the garden.
25. The telephone is on the table.
26. The apples are in the bag.
27. The kitchen is clean.
28. Is the bar open?
29. All the windows and doors are closed.
30. The books are on the sofa.

13. DESCRIPTIONS - ESTAR

MASCULINE AND FEMININE ADJECTIVES.

As we have seen, all nouns in Spanish are masculine or feminine. As a consequence of this, adjectives, i.e. describing words, including colours take an ending appropriate to their gender.

E.g. **El** chico está cansado   **La** chica está cansada
     El coche está sucio   **La casa está sucia**

Also, they have to become plural if they are describing a plural noun.
E,g   **Los** chicos están cansados   **Las** chicas están cansadas
     Los coches están sucios   **Las** casas están sucias

If the nouns described are a mixture of masculine and feminine, for example:
John and Jane are married - John y Jane están casados

PRACTICE A: TRANSLATE

1. The doors and windows are open.
2. The floor in her house is never dirty.
3. The people are very angry.
4. We are very sad because they are ill.
5. At last the kitchen is clean.
6. You(s) are always happy on Fridays.
7. Pedro is married but Carmen is divorced.
8. The chair is free at the moment.
9. I am more comfortable in my old shoes.
10. They are not comfortable with the situation.
11. Are you ill?
12. María has a cold but Paco is fine.
13. Maite and Dulce are both very happy in their work.
14. We are uncomfortable today because we are cold.
15. They are angry with us today.

14. THE VERB "ESTAR" IN CONTEXT - EN LA CLASE

PRACTICE A: Practice saying this conversation out loud.

Pablo: Buenos días, Carmen. ¿Cómo estás?
Carmen: Estoy muy bien, gracias, ¿y tú?
Pablo: Estoy muy bien también. ¿Dónde está tu hermana María?
Carmen: No está en clase hoy, está en la casa.
Pablo: ¿Por qué? ¿Está enferma?
Carmen: Si. Está resfriada.
Pablo: ¿Dónde está la casa?
Carmen: Está en Calle San Juan, número 18, a la izquierda de la calle.
Pablo: Gracias.

(En la casa de María)

Pablo: Hola María, ¿cómo estás?
María: Estoy resfriada, pero hoy estoy un poco mejor.
Pablo: Me gusta tu casa, es muy bonita.
María: Si, pero hoy está muy desordenada. ¿Está abierta la puerta? Tengo frio, no estoy cómoda.
Pablo: Si, la puerta está abierta. Ahora está cerrada. ¿Estás cómoda ahora?
María: Si, ahora estoy muy bien.

PRACTICE B. Find the 20 examples of the verb "estar" in this text and the one example of "ser".

PRACTICE C: Translate the text into English.

PRACTICE D: Translate the questions into Spanish and then answer in Spanish. N.B. remember to use the correct verb endings.

1. How is Carmen?
2. Where is her sister María?
3. Is she ill?
4. Where is the house?
5. How is María today?
6. What is the house like?
7. What is it like today?
8. Is María comfortable?
9. Why is she cold?
10. Is she comfortable now?
11. How are you today?
12. Are you comfortable?

Top Tips!!

---

6. Apostrophe "s"- Remember-

Although in English we use the apostrophe plus "s" to signify possession (John´s car, Carol´s mother) -This does not in fact exist in any other language. In Spanish we have to say:
"The car of John"- El coche de Juan.
"The mother of Carol"-La madre de Carol.

---

7. "a" plus profession.

In Spanish it is not neccesary to translate "a" when we are talking about someone´s profession.

E.g. Soy profesora- I am a teacher.
      Es médico- He is a doctor.
      Eres estudiante de español- You are a Spanish student.

---

8. Making negatives.

To make a negative in Spanish, we simply place "no" directly before the verb.

   E.g. No soy profesora- I am not a
                          teacher.
    No estamos felices- We are not
                        happy.

15. TRANSLATION ENGLISH TO SPANISH- "ESTAR"

PRACTICE A- Practice reading this text out loud and then translate into Spanish.

IN THE CLASS

Pedro: Good day. Pablo. How are you?
Pablo: I am very good thanks, and you?
Pedro: I am ill. I have a cold.
Pablo: Why aren't you in the house? Where is your house?
Pedro: I have an English class. My house is on Cartagena Street, number 13, on the right.
Pablo: I have an English class too. I like the class very much it is very interesting.
Pedro: Yes but when the window is open I am cold.
Pablo: It is closed today. Are you comfortable?
Pedro: Yes I am very comfortable thank you. And you?
Pablo: Yes, me too.

PRACTICE B: Translate the questions into Spanish and then answer in Spanish.

1. How is Pedro?
2. Why is he not in the house?
3. How is Pablo?
4. Where is Pedro´s house?
5. What is the class like?
6. Is the window open or closed?
7. How are you today?
8. Are you comfortable?

16. CONVERSATION PRACTICE- "ESTAR" ONLY

PRACTICE A: Translate these questions into Spanish and answer in Spanish.

1. Where are you?

2. Are you married?

3. Where is Barcelona?

4. Are you tired?

5. Are you happy?

6. What colour is the sky today?

7. How are you?

8. Are you ill?

9. Where is Buckingham Palace?

10. Where is the Spanish class?

11. When are you sad?

12. When are you happy?

17. COPPPRINCT/ FLOMMETS- The difference between "ser" and "estar"

"SER"- "COPPPRINCT"

C OLOURS
O RIGIN
P ROFESSION
P OSSESSION
P ERSONAL
R ELATIONSHIPS
I DENTITY
N ATIONALITY
C HARACTERISTICS
T IME

"ESTAR"- "FLOMMETS"

F EELINGS
L
O CATION
M OODS
M ARITAL STATUS
E MOTIONS
T EMPORARY
S TATES

18. SER AND ESTAR- CONVERSATION PRACTICE

Translate these questions into Spanish and answer them in Spanish.

1. Where are you from?
2. Where is your house?
3. What is your house like?
4. When is Christmas?
5. Where is Madrid?
6. Why is Spanish important for you?
7. What is Spain like?
8. Who is your best friend?
9. Where is your car?
10. When is your birthday?
11. Are you tired?
12. Are you happy?
13. What colour is your car?
14. What day is it?
15. Who are you with?
16. Which is better, Spain or Great Britain?
17. Are you at home?
18. When is the Spanish class?
19. Who is the President of Spain?
20. Is the sky grey today?

19. HAY

Hay is a really useful word in Spanish, translating to "there is", "there are", "is there", or "are there"
For example, you might say:

En mi jardín <u>hay</u> una piscina- In my garden <u>there is</u> a swimming pool. En el parque <u>hay</u> muchos árboles- In the park <u>there are</u> many trees.

Also you can use it to ask questions:

E.g ¿<u>Hay</u> muchas personas en la fiesta? <u>Are there</u> many people at the party?
¿<u>Hay</u> leche en el frigorifico? <u>Is there</u> any milk in the fridge? (n.b it is not neccessary to translate "any".)

To make the negative, simply put "no" before "hay".

E.g <u>No hay</u> árboles en mi jardín- <u>There are no</u> trees in my garden

PRACTICE A: Translate the following questions into Spanish and answer them in Spanish using "hay"

1. How many bedrooms are there in your house?

2. Is there a television in your bedroom?

3. Are there any flowers in your garden?

4. Are there pictures in your living room?

5. Are there any animals in your house?

6. How many trees are there in your garden?

7. Are there any good restaurants near your house?

8. Are there many books in your house?

9. Is there a car in front of your house?

10. What is there on your bedside table?

20. HAY/ ESTAR/ SER

PRACTICE A: Find the English meaning of these words.

1-HAY

UNA MESA
UNA SILLA
UNA VENTANA
UN CUADRO
UNA LÁMPARA
UNA RADIO
UNA ALFOMBRA
UN SILLÓN

UNA REVISTA
UN PERIÓDICO
UNA TELEVISIÓN
UN LIBRO
UNA LUZ
UN SOFÁ
UNA ESTANTERÍA
UN ARMARIO

2-ESTÁ / ESTÁN

A LA DERECHA/ IZQUIERDA
SOBRE
EN
ENCIMA DE
DELANTE DE
DETRÁS DE
AL LADO DE

EN EL CENTRO DE
EN EL RINCÓN
ALREDEDOR DE
DEBAJO DE
ENTRE
EN LA PARED
CERCA DE FUERA

3-ES /SON

ALTO/A/S
BAJO/A/S
LARGO/A/S
GRANDE/S
REDONDO/A/S

RECTANGULO/A/S
ESTRECHO/A/S
CUADRADO/A/S
PEQUEÑO/A/S
ANCHO/A/S

PRACTICE B: Use them to describe the picture. Use at least 150 words.
E.g. En la sala hay 2 sofás. Los sofás están en el centro de la sala. etc.

21. DESCRIBING PEOPLE

As we saw earlier, descriptions of people or objects have to match up with the gender and number of the same. In this section we are going to concentrate on descriptions of people, below is some vocabulary you will find useful.

¿Cómo es?   What is he/she like?
¿Cómo son? What are they like?

PRACTICE A: Listen to these descriptions and practice saying them.

ES/SON - is/are (INTRINSIC CHARACTERISTICS we use the verb "SER")

alto/a/s – tall   simpático/a/s- nice
moreno/a/s - dark   bajo/a/s – short
antipático/a/s – unpleasant cantante/s -singer
guapo/a/s - good-looking   delgado/a/s – slim
actor-actor   feo/a/s – ugly
rubio/a/s – blonde   actríz -actress
gordo/a/s – fat   calvo/a – bald
político/a/s- politician

ESTÁ/ESTÁN - is/are (MARITAL STATUS we use the verb "ESTAR")

casado/a/s-married   separado/a/s-separated
soltero/a/s-single   viudo/a/s-widowed
divorciado/a/s-divorced

TIENE/TIENEN - he/she has (we use the verb "TENER"-see chapter 24)

<u>ojos</u> - eyes   <u>pelo</u> - hair   others
<u>azules</u> – blue   rubio - blonde   <u>hijos</u> - children
<u>verdes</u> - green   <u>moreno</u> - dark   <u>años</u> – years
<u>grises</u> - grey   negro-black
<u>castaños</u> - brown   gris - grey
                           <u>blanco</u>-white
                           <u>liso</u> - straight
                           <u>rizado</u> - curly
                           largo - long
                           <u>corto</u> - short
                           <u>ondulado</u> - wavy

22. ¿QUIÉN ES?/ ¿QUIENES SON? - Who is it?/ Who are they?

PRACTICE A: Translate into English and guess who it is.

1. Es americano. Es bilionario. Tiene pelo moreno y corta. Es bastante alto con ojos castaños. Es hombre de negocios y el propietario de Twitter. Tiene más menos 55 años y está divorciado tres veces ¿Quién es?

2. Es americano. Está muerto. Es negro con pelo largo y rizado. Es muy delgado y es cantante y baila muy bien. Tiene cuatro niños adoptivos. Tiene cincuenta años. Tiene muchos hermanos. ¿Quién es?

3. Es inglés. No es muy alto. Es casi calvo y tiene orejas grandes. Tiene ojos azules. Es muy rico. Está casado y tiene dos hijos. Lleva una corona. Su familia es Real. Tiene más o menos setenta años. Habla con plantas y árboles y sus hijos son príncipes. ¿Quién es?

PRACTICE B: Think of a famous <u>man</u>, and write a brief description using the above as a guide. Remember to use masculine descriptions where appropriate. Then read it out to someone who speaks Spanish to see if they can guess who it is.

PRACTICE C: Read and translate the following <u>feminine</u> descriptions and guess who they are.

1-Es americana. Es morena, con pelo corto y ojos castaños. Tiene más o menos sesenta años. Es muy alta, delgada y guapa. Está casada con un pólitico muy famoso. Tiene dos hijas. ¿Quién es?

2-Es americana, guapa y morena con pelo largo y liso. Está divorciada de actor americano muy famoso y tienen muchos niños adoptivos. Su padre también es actor famoso, Jon Voight. Tiene más o menos cincuenta. Es famosa por sus labios grandes. ¿Quién es?

3-Es americana, tiene más o menos treinta y cinco años. Es rubia, delgada y guapa. Es actor y cantante. Está divorciada y no tiene hijos. Canta "Felíz Cumpleaños" al Presidente. Está muerta. ¿Quién es?

PRACTICE D: Think of a famous <u>woman</u> and write a brief description using the above as a guide. Remember to use <u>feminine</u> descriptions where appropriate. Then read it out to someone who speaks Spanish to see if they can guess who it is.

PRACTICE E: Read and translate the following plural descriptions and guess who they are.

1-Son actores. No son guapos. Uno es alto, delgado y rubio. Es inglés. El otro también es alto, pero gordo y calvo. Él es americano. Son cómicos. Siempre llevan trajes y sombreros negros. Sus películas son de blanco y negro. **¿Quiénes son?**

2-Están casados. Son ingleses. Él es alto, guapo y delgado. Tiene pelo rubio y muy corto. Ella es baja, muy delgada, morena con pelo moreno. Es muy guapa. Él es futbolista y ella es mujer de negocios ahora, antes cantante. Tienen 4 hijos. Tienen más o menos 50 años. **¿Quiénes son?**

3-Están casados y tienen dos hijos. Él es inglés y ella es americana. Ella es actor, él es de familia real. Tienen más o menos 35 años. Viven en los Estado Unidos. El es pelirrojo con ojos azules y ella es morena con ojos castaños. Los dos son guapos.
¿Quiénes son?

PRACTICE F: Think of a famous group or pair of people, for example a double act, a married couple or a band. Write a brief description using the above as a guide. Remember to use masculine, feminine or plural descriptions where appropriate. Then read it out to someone who speaks Spanish to see if they can guess who it is.

23. LA CASA DE PEDRO

PRACTICE A: Practice reading this out loud.

Pedro Martínez es español. Es de Alicante. Es mecánico. ¿Dónde está hoy? Hoy está en casa. En la casa hay dos dormitorios, un cuarto de baño, una cocina, un comedor y una sala. Pedro está en la sala. ¿Cómo es la sala? Es muy grande. En la sala hay una mesa, un sofá, un sillón, unas sillas y una television. Sobre el suelo hay una alfombra. Un perro está sentado en la alfombra debajo de una silla. La madre de Pedro está sentada en el sillón. El sillón es muy cómodo. Pedro está sentado en el sofá. ¿Qué hay sobre la mesa? Sobre la mesa hay una taza y en la taza hay café. También hay una revista y unos libros. Sobre la pared hay un espejo y unos cuadros. La televisión está debajo del espejo.

PRACTICE B: Pick out all the examples of "es" or "está" you find and think about why they are "ser" or "estar".

PRACTICE C: Translate the text into English.

PRACTICE D: Translate the questions below into Spanish and then answer them in Spanish.

1. Where is Pedro from?
2. What is Pedro?
3. Where is he today?
4. How many bedrooms are there in the house?
5. What is the living room like?
6. What is there on the floor?
7. Where is Pedro´s mother?
8. What is there on the table?
9. Where are the pictures?
10. Where is the television?

 Top Tips!!

9. Question Words

1. ¿Quién? -Who?

2. ¿Qué? –What?

3. ¿Dónde? - Where?

4. ¿Por qué? -Why?

5. ¿Cuál? - Which?

6. ¿Cuándo? - When?

7. ¿Cómo? - How?

10. Order of Questions

If there is a preposition in the question (with, to, at etc) this comes first, followed by the question word, followed by the verb, followed by the subject (the person or thing that the verb refers to).
E.g. ¿Con quién está Carmen?- Who is Carmen with?
¿A qué hora es la fiesta?- At what time is the party?

24. REGULAR VERBS - 1ST CONJUGATION – 'AR' VERBS

A verb is a "doing" word. In English all verbs in their original form, or infinitive, are preceded by "to". "To dance" "to eat" "to drink" "to buy" are all verbs that have not yet been conjugated and therefore do not refer to any person. These are known as "infinitives".

In Spanish, there are 3 kinds of verbs, whether regular or irregular. A regular verb is one that follows a universal pattern, whereas an irregular verb has a unique structure.

All Spanish verbs in their infinitive, or original form, end in either 'ar', 'er' or 'ir'. These are known as the **1st, 2nd and 3rd conjugation.**

HABLAR – to speak

If we look at this verb in the present tense in English first, it conjugates as follows:

PERSON	TO SPEAK (INFINITIVE)
1st person singular	I speak
2nd person singular	You speak
3rd person singular	He/she/it speaks
1st person plural	We speak
2nd person plural	You (s) speak
3rd person plural	They speak

We can see that there is only one verb change in English 'speaks' for the 3rd person. Now let's do the same thing in Spanish.

First, we remove the ending of the verb, the 'ar', which leaves us with the stem or root of the verb. We then add back different endings to indicate which person we wish to express.

PERSON	TO SPEAK (INFINITIVE)	HABLAR (INFINITIVE)
1st person singular	I speak	(yo) hablo
2nd person singular	You speak	(tú) hablas
3rd person singular	He/she/it speaks	(Él/ella) habla
1st person plural	We speak	(nosotros/as) hablamos
2nd person plural	You (s) speak	(vosotros/as) habláis
3rd person plural	They speak	(ellos/as) hablan

PRACTICE A: All the following verbs are regular 'ar' verbs and follow the same pattern. Find their meanings in your dictionary and conjugate them in the boxes:

1. Andar

(yo)	
(tú)	
(él/ella)	
(nosotros/nosotras)	
(vosotros/as)	
(ellos/ellas)	

2. Bailar

(yo)	
(tú)	
(él/ella)	
(nosotros/nosotras)	
(vosotros/as)	
(ellos/ellas)	

3. Buscar

(yo)	
(tú)	
(él/ella)	
(nosotros/nosotras)	
(vosotros/as)	
(ellos/ellas)	

4. Cantar

(yo)	
(tú)	
(él/ella)	
(nosotros/nosotras)	
(vosotros/as)	
(ellos/ellas)	

5. Estudiar

(yo)	
(tú)	
(él/ella)	
(nosotros/nosotras)	
(vosotros/as)	
(ellos/ellas)	

6. Comprar

(yo)	
(tú)	
(él/ella)	
(nosotros/nosotras)	
(vosotros/as)	
(ellos/ellas)	

7. Escuchar

(yo)	
(tú)	
(él/ella)	
(nosotros/nosotras)	
(vosotros/as)	
(ellos/ellas)	

8. Esperar

(yo)	
(tú)	
(él/ella)	
(nosotros/nosotras)	
(vosotros/as)	
(ellos/ellas)	

9. Llegar

(yo)	
(tú)	
(él/ella)	
(nosotros/nosotras)	
(vosotros/as)	
(ellos/ellas)	

10. Mirar

(yo)	
(tú)	
(él/ella)	
(nosotros/nosotras)	
(vosotros/as)	
(ellos/ellas)	

11. Llevar

(yo)	
(tú)	
(él/ella)	
(nosotros/nosotras)	
(vosotros/as)	
(ellos/ellas)	

12. Practicar

(yo)	
(tú)	
(él/ella)	
(nosotros/nosotras)	
(vosotros/as)	
(ellos/ellas)	

13. Preparar

(yo)	
(tú)	
(él/ella)	
(nosotros/nosotras)	
(vosotros/as)	
(ellos/ellas)	

14. Trabajar

(yo)	
(tú)	
(él/ella)	
(nosotros/nosotras)	
(vosotros/as)	
(ellos/ellas)	

15. Tocar

(yo)	
(tú)	
(él/ella)	
(nosotros/nosotras)	
(vosotros/as)	
(ellos/ellas)	

PRACTICE B: Translate (each sentence uses one of the above verbs).

1. They play the guitar.
2. She practises every day.
3. He prepares the contract.
4. Carlos is wearing trousers and a T-shirt.
5. I work in a bank.
6. We always sing in the bath.

7. You(s) walk to the school.
8. I dance every Saturday.
9. She is looking for her dog.
10. We study Spanish in El Príncipe.
11. I buy meat in the supermarket.
12. He listens to the radio every day.
13. They arrive on Friday.
14. You are waiting for the bus.
15. I look at the house.

MAKING QUESTIONS-

In Spanish, when we make a question, it is not necessary to translate 'do', 'does', 'are' or 'is'. For example:

Do you speak Spanish? –
¿Hablas español?
What are you waiting for? –
¿Qué esperas?

We can see that this almost seems too simple!!

We often want to make things more complicated in an 'English' way.

PRACTICE C: Find the meaning of the question words below and make questions to fit the statements you translated earlier.

For example:

1. They play the guitar - **Tocan la guitarra.**
A relevant question could be: What do they play? - **¿Qué tocan?**

QUESTION WORDS

1. ¿Qué?
2. ¿Cómo?
3. ¿Cuándo?
4. ¿Por qué?
5. ¿Quién?
6. ¿Dónde?
7. ¿Cuál?

PRACTICE D: Conversation Practice. Using the 'ar' verbs we have looked at and the question words, translate these questions into Spanish looking up any words you don´t know in the dictionary.

1. What languages do you speak?
2. When do you dance?
3. Do you sing on karaoke?
4. Where do you study Spanish?
5. When do you practice Spanish?
6. Where do you work?
7. How do you prepare a tortilla?
8. What music do you listen to on the radio?
9. Where do you buy clothes?
10. Are you looking for a new car?
11. What are you wearing?
12. Do you walk to work?
13. What instruments do you play?
14. When do you watch the television?

Top Tips!!

---

11. "Al" and "Del"
When the preposition "a" is followed by "el" they contract and become "al".
E.g Ando al supermercado- I walk to the supermarket. The same happens with "de" and "el".
E.g Ando del supermercado- I walk from the supermarket.

---

12. "at"

In Spanish we normally use "en" (in) rather than "a" (at) for places.
E.g. Estoy en la playa- I am at the beach. Estamos en casa- We are at home

25. 'AR' VERBS IN CONTEXT

Pedro y María son españoles pero ahora están en Inglaterra. Están en la Universidad de Manchester. Pedro estudia inglés y María estudia inglés también. Estudian mucho y son muy buenos estudiantes.

María habla inglés perfectamente, y también habla francés, español y un poco de alemán. Practica todos los días en la Universidad y con los amigos. Pedro habla inglés perfectamente también, pero no habla francés ni alemán. Él practica mucho con los otros estudiantes y sus amigos.

Los sábados, los dos trabajan. Pedro trabaja en una oficina y María trabaja en una tienda. Ganan dinero para comprar ropa y comida y pagar el alquiler. Todos los días andan a la Universidad. Su casa está muy cerca.

Las tardes, después de las clases, estudian un poco, practican el inglés con los amigos y luego miran la tele en casa. Pedro prepara la cena y María toca la guitarra. Después de cenar, escuchan la radio, y hablan solamente en inglés para practicar más.

PRACTICE A: Find the 30 verbs in this text and use them to fill out the verb identification table below.

VERB IN CONTEXT	INFINITIVE	ENGLISH	PERSON
1. son	ser	To be	3rd p plural
2.			
3.			
4.			
5.			
6.			
7.			
8.			
9.			
10.			
11.			
12.			
13.			
14.			
15.			

16.				
17.				
18.				
19.				
20.				
21.				
22.				
23.				
24.				
25.				
26.				
27.				
28.				
29.				
30.				

PRACTICE B: Translate the text into English.

PRACTICE C: Translate these questions into Spanish then answer in Spanish from the text.

1. Where are Pedro and María from?
2. Where are they now?
3. What does Pedro study?
4. Who studies English also?
5. What languages does María also speak?
6. When does she practice?
7. Do they both work?
8. Who works in a shop?
9. Why do they earn money?
10. How do they get to university?
11. When do they watch the television?
12. Who prepares the dinner?
13. What instrument does María play?
14. Why do they only speak in English?

Top Tips!!

13. Time- "Tiempo", "vez" or "hora"?

The word "time" in Spanish causes much confusion.
We use "tiempo" for a period of time:
E.g. Mucho tiempo- a long time
"Vez" is used for the number of times you do something:
E.g. Visito la playa una vez por semana- I visit the beach once (one time) a week.
"Hora" is used for clock time:
E.g. ¿Qué hora es?- What time is it?

14. "Hablar" plus "con".

In Spanish, we normally speak "with" people rather than "to" them.
E.g. Hablo con Juan- I speak to Juan

As "con" is a preposition, in a question it starts the sentence.

E.g. ¿Con quién hablas?- Who do you speak to?

15. "ing" words

Gerunds or "ing" words are not used so commonly in Spanish as they are in English. The simple present tense is used in their place. Therefore, the example above ¿Con quién hablas? Could also translate to Who are you speaking to? as well as Who do you speak to?

26. REGULAR VERBS – 2ᴺᴰ CONJUGATION – 'ER' VERBS

Just like with 'ar' verbs, to conjugate 'er' verbs we first remove the ending from the infinitive, leaving us with the root or stem. We then add back an appropriate ending for each.

PERSON	TO EAT (INFINITIVE)	COMER (INFINITIVE)
1ˢᵗ person singular	I eat	(yo) como
2ⁿᵈ person singular	You eat	(tú) com<u>es</u>
3ʳᵈ person singular	He/she/it eats	(Él/ella) come
1ˢᵗ person plural	We eat	(nosotros/as) com<u>emos</u>
2ⁿᵈ person plural	You (s) eat	(vosotros/as) com<u>éis</u>
3ʳᵈ person plural	They eat	(ellos/as) com<u>en</u>

PRACTICE A: Find the meaning of these other regular 'er' verbs and conjugate them accordingly in the boxes provided.

1. Beber

(yo)	
(tú)	
(él/ella)	
(nosotros/nosotras)	
(vosotros/as)	
(ellos/ellas)	

2. Aprender

(yo)	
(tú)	
(él/ella)	
(nosotros/nosotras)	
(vosotros/as)	
(ellos/ellas)	

3. creer

(yo)	
(tú)	
(él/ella)	
(nosotros/nosotras)	
(vosotros/as)	
(ellos/ellas)	

4. vender

(yo)	
(tú)	
(él/ella)	
(nosotros/nosotras)	
(vosotros/as)	
(ellos/ellas)	

5. leer

(yo)	
(tú)	
(él/ella)	
(nosotros/nosotras)	
(vosotros/as)	
(ellos/ellas)	

6. comprender

(yo)	
(tú)	
(él/ella)	
(nosotros/nosotras)	
(vosotros/as)	
(ellos/ellas)	

7. correr

(yo)	
(tú)	
(él/ella)	
(nosotros/nosotras)	
(vosotros/as)	
(ellos/ellas)	

8. deber

(yo)	
(tú)	
(él/ella)	
(nosotros/nosotras)	
(vosotros/as)	
(ellos/ellas)	

9. romper

(yo)	
(tú)	
(él/ella)	
(nosotros/nosotras)	
(vosotros/as)	
(ellos/ellas)	

10. ver (n.b. slightly irregular-leave on the "e" for 1st person singular.)

(yo)	
(tú)	
(él/ella)	
(nosotros/nosotras)	
(vosotros/as)	
(ellos/ellas)	

PRACTICE B: Translate these sentences into Spanish.

1. I often have lunch in a Spanish restaurant.
2. I drink milk every day.
3. I do not understand Russian.
4. I read a lot of books.
5. I learn a lot of Spanish on the internet.

6. Manuel sells clothes at the market.
7. Carmen always runs in the marathon.
8. We believe in UFOs.
9. A lot of Americans understand Spanish.
10. They must learn Spanish.
11. I break something every day.
12. He watches the television at weekends.
13. He always drinks beer in the bar.
14. We must eat more vegetables.
15. Normally, they sell cars but in the summer they sell houses.

PRACTICE C: Conversation Practice. Translate these questions into Spanish and answer.

1. What do you see from your bedroom window?
2. Why must you study Spanish?
3. Do you understand Spanish verbs?
4. What do you drink in a restaurant?
5. Do you believe in ghosts?
6. Are you selling your house?
7. Do you break many things?
8. Do you read many books?
9. Where do you normally have lunch on Sundays?
10. Do you eat a lot of vegetables?
11. When do you drink alcohol in the house?
12. When do you run?
13. Why do you learn Spanish?
14. Why must you drink water in the summer?

27. 'ER' VERBS IN CONTEXT

Pedro y María **están** en un restaurante español en el centro de la ciudad de Manchester.

María bebe vino tinto y Pedro bebe cerveza. María lee una revista y Pedro lee un periódico. Comprenden muchas de las palabras en inglés pero no todas.

Aprenden mucho inglés con sus amigos ingleses, pero también aprenden mucho cuando leen periódicos y revistas, y cuando ven la tele por la noche. Creen que el inglés es muy importante para su futuro.

Pedro ve un anuncio en el periódico, un chico vende una bicicleta. Los dos creen que deben comprar esta bicicleta para hacer más ejercicio.

De primero, los dos comen ensalada. De segundo, María come paella y Pedro come macarrones. De postre, Pedro come flan y María come arroz con leche. Después de comer, los dos beben café con leche.

Terminan de comer a las cuatro más o menos. Cuando pagan la cuenta, Pedro rompe un vaso que está en la mesa. El camarero no está enfadado, y los dos corren a la parada del autobús porque ahora es tarde y deben coger el autobús a las cuatro y cuarto.

PRACTICE A: *Find the 35 verbs in this text and fill out the table below as per the example.*

VERB	INFINITIVE	ENGLISH	PERSON
1. están	estar	To be	3rd p. plural
2.			
3.			
4.			
5.			
6.			
7.			
8.			
9.			
10.			
11.			
12.			
13.			
14			
15.			
16.			

17.				
18.				
19.				
20.				
21.				
22.				
23.				
24.				
25.				
26.				
27.				
28.				
29.				
30.				
31.				
32.				
33.				
34.				
35.				

PRACTICE B: *Translate the text into English.*

PRACTICE C: *Translate these questions into Spanish then answer in Spanish from the text.*

1. Where are Pedro and María?
2. What is María drinking?
3. Who is drinking beer?
4. What are they reading?
5. When do they learn a lot of English?
6. Why do they believe that English is very important?
7. What does Pedro see in the newspaper?
8. What is the boy selling?
9. What do they both eat for starter?
10. Who eats paella for the main course?
11. What does Pedro eat for dessert?
12. What do they both drink after eating?
13. What does Pedro break when they pay the bill?
14. Is the waiter angry?
15. Why do they run to the bus stop?
16. What time must they catch the bus?

 Top Tips!!

16. "On" Monday, Tuesday etc

When we say "on" a certain day or days in Spanish, we do not use "en".
We use "el" if it is one particular day:
E.g. Llegan el Jueves- They arrive on
Thursday And the plural "los" if it is more
than one day:
E.g. Los sábados trabajo en una tienda- On Saturdays I work in a shop.

17. "Para"- In order to.

"Para" has many uses in Spanish and one is to say "in order to do something".
Although in English this can often be omitted:

E.g. I work (in order) to live, in Spanish it is always necessary. "Trabajo para vivir", never "Trabajo vivir", even though vivir can translate to "to live"

18. The personal "a".

When the action or verb in a sentence is performed on a person, the preposition "a" is always necessary, although not in English.
E.g. Visito a mi abuela- I visit my grandmother
In a question, this comes first as with all prepositions.
E.g. ¿A quién visitas?- Who do you visit?

28. REGULAR VERBS – 3ʳᴰ CONJUGATION – 'IR' VERBS

'Ir' verbs are the third and final conjugation in Spanish. Again, we begin by removing the ending leaving us with the root or 'stem', then we add back on an appropriate ending.

PERSON	TO LIVE (INFINITIVE)	VIVIR (INFINITIVE)
1ˢᵗ person singular	I live	(yo) vivo
2ⁿᵈ person singular	You live	(tú) vives
3ʳᵈ person singular	He/she/it lives	(Él/ella) vive
1ˢᵗ person plural	We live	(nosotros/as) vivimos
2ⁿᵈ person plural	You (s) live	(vosotros/as) vivís
3ʳᵈ person plural	They live	(ellos/as) viven

PRACTICE A: Find the meaning of these other regular 'ir' verbs and conjugate them as above.

1. escribir

(yo)	
(tú)	
(él/ella)	
(nosotros/nosotras)	
(vosotros/as)	
(ellos/ellas)	

2. recibir

(yo)	
(tú)	
(él/ella)	
(nosotros/nosotras)	
(vosotros/as)	
(ellos/ellas)	

3. cubrir

(yo)	
(tú)	
(él/ella)	
(nosotros/nosotras)	
(vosotros/as)	
(ellos/ellas)	

4. subir

(yo)	
(tú)	
(él/ella)	
(nosotros/nosotras)	
(vosotros/as)	
(ellos/ellas)	

5. descubrir

(yo)	
(tú)	
(él/ella)	
(nosotros/nosotras)	
(vosotros/as)	
(ellos/ellas)	

6. compartir

(yo)	
(tú)	
(él/ella)	
(nosotros/nosotras)	
(vosotros/as)	
(ellos/ellas)	

7. sufrir

(yo)	
(tú)	
(él/ella)	
(nosotros/nosotras)	
(vosotros/as)	
(ellos/ellas)	

8. repartir

(yo)	
(tú)	
(él/ella)	
(nosotros/nosotras)	
(vosotros/as)	
(ellos/ellas)	

9. abrir

(yo)	
(tú)	
(él/ella)	
(nosotros/nosotras)	
(vosotros/as)	
(ellos/ellas)	

10. discutir

(yo)	
(tú)	
(él/ella)	
(nosotros/nosotras)	
(vosotros/as)	
(ellos/ellas)	

PRACTICE B: Translate into Spanish.

1. Do you write many emails?
2. In Africa, many children suffer.
3. The snow covers the mountains.
4. I get on the train in Barcelona.
5. We always discover the truth in the end.
6. The teacher hands out the exams.
7. Juan and Pedro share a flat in Madrid.
8. Do you(s) receive many letters?
9. He always opens the door for me.
10. They argue every Saturday evening.

26. TRANSLATION FROM ENGLISH TO SPANISH - REGULAR VERBS

PRACTICE A: Identify the 17 verbs in this text

Marcos lives in Benidorm with his family. He works in a bank, and on Wednesday evenings he studies English at a private school. He watches the TV on Mondays, and on Tuesdays he speaks to his English friends. He does not understand everything.

On Thursdays he reads history books, and on Fridays he visits a local bar. He always drinks red wine and eats tapas. On Saturdays he sells chickens at the market, and on Sundays he writes emails to his friends in England. He learns a lot of English with them.

Marcos is tall, dark and has brown eyes. He is very nice and shares everything with his family.

PRACTICE B: Translate the text into Spanish. NB: When we say "on" a certain day in Spanish, we use "el" if it is one particular day (on Saturday = el sábado), or "los" if it is on a regular basis (on Saturdays = los sabados).

PRACTICE C: Now translate the following questions into Spanish and answer them in Spanish.

1. Where does Marcos live and who with?
2. Where does he work?
3. What does he study on Wednesday evenings?
4. Where does he study?
5. What does he do on Mondays?
6. Who does he speak to on Tuesdays?
7. Does he understand everything?
8. What does he read on Thursdays?
9. What does he always eat and drink at his local bar on Fridays?
10. What does he sell at the market on Saturdays?
11. Who does he write to on Sundays?
12. What is Marcos like?

30. ADVERBS OF FREQUENCY

PRACTICE A: Find the equivalent word or expression in Spanish in a dictionary.

1. ALWAYS
2. OFTEN
3. NORMALLY
4. SOMETIMES
5. NEARLY NEVER
6. NEVER
7. ONCE IN A WHILE
8. ONCE A WEEK
9. ONCE A MONTH
10. ONCE A YEAR
11. EVERY DAY
12. EVERY WEEK
13. EVERY MONTH
14. EVERY SATURDAY
15. EVERY MORNING
16. EVERY EVENING

PRACTICE B: Now write a sentence using the verbs you have learnt so far for each adverb of frequency.

For example:

A menudo como chocolate.

Nunca bebo té por la mañana.

31. CONVERSATION PRACTICE REGULAR VERBS.

Translate these questions into Spanish and answer in Spanish.

1. What languages do you speak?
2. Where do you live?
3. When do you dance?
4. Do you open the window in your bedroom at night?
5. What do you drink in a restaurant?
6. Do you believe in ghosts?
7. Do you sing on karaoke?
8. When do you practice Spanish?
9. Where do you work?
10. When do you drink alcohol in the house?
11. When do you run?
12. What music do you listen to on the radio?
13. Where do you buy clothes?
14. Do you receive a lot of letters?
15. Do you break many things?
16. Do you read many books?
17. What are you wearing?
18. Do you walk every day?
19. What instruments do you play?
20. When do you watch the television?
21. Where do you speak Spanish?
22. Why must you study Spanish?
23. Do you walk to the beach?
24. Do you understand Spanish verbs?

32. PRACTICE OF REGULAR VERBS

PRACTICE A: Practice reading this text out loud.

Mí nombre **es** Pablo García. Nosotros **vivimos** en Alicante, en la Calle Ramón y Cajal, número 13. Mi padre trabaja en un banco y mi madre trabaja en el colegio. Trabajan de lunes a viernes. Mi padre sale de la casa a las 8 y mi madre a las 9. Mi padre coge el autobús y mi madre coge el tren.

Yo estudio inglés en la Universidad. Nunca regreso a casa a mediodía, como en el comedor del campus con mis compañeros. Mis padres comen en el trabajo.

Mi hermana no trabaja hasta la noche. Ella ordena la casa, prepara las comidas, lava la ropa o plancha.

Regresamos a casa sobre las 5 o 6. Mi padre lee el periódico, mi madre mira la television o lee un libro. Mi hermana canta en un bar cerca de la casa y no cena con nosotros. Muchas veces, después de cenar, estudio hasta las doce de la noche. Mis padres miran la tele, escuchan la radio o preparan las cosas para la mañana.

PRACTICE B: Find the 28 verbs in this text. Then copy them into the verb recognition table below. The first two have been done for you.

	VERB IN CONTEXT	INFINITIVE	ENGLISH	MEANING IN CONTEXT	PERSON
1	es	ser	to be	is	3rd person singular
2	vivimos	vivir	to live	we live	1st person plural
3					
4					
5					
6					
7					
8					
9					
10					
11					
12					
13					
14					

15					
16					
17					
18					
19					
20					
21					
22					
23					
24					
25					
26					
27					
28					

PRACTICE C: Translate the text into English.

PRACTICE D: Translate the following questions into Spanish and then answer in Spanish. The answers are all in the text.

1. Where do Pablo García and his family live?
2. Where do his mother and father work?
3. What days do they work?
4. What time do they leave the house?
5. What does his father catch?
6. And his mother?
7. Does Pablo work?
8. What does he study?
9. Where does he study?
10. Does he return home at midday?
11. Where does he have lunch?
12. Where do his parents have lunch?
13. Does his sister work?
14. What does she do in the house?
15. What time do they return home?
16. What do his mother and father do then?
17. Where does his sister sing?
18. Does she dine with them?
19. What does Pablo do after dinner?
20. What do his parents do?

33. DIPHTHONGS - ROOT OR STEM CHANGING VERBS

There are groups of Spanish Verbs that are regular in their endings but change their stems in the present tense.

DIPTHONGS 1. The first group are verbs that change from **o** to **ue**.
E.g. contar - to count

PERSON	TO COUNT (INFINITIVE)	CONTAR (INFINITIVE)
1st person singular	I count	(yo) cuento
2nd person singular	You count	(tú) cuentas
3rd person singular	He/she/it counts	(Él/ella) cuenta
1st person plural	We count	(nosotros/as) contamos*
2nd person plural	You (s) count	(vosotros/as) contáis*
3rd person plural	They count	(ellos/as) cuentan

*The stem changes in the 1st, 2nd and 3rd person singular, and the 3rd person plural, but **NOT** in the 1st and 2nd person plural. The endings are regular, conditional on whether it is an 'ar', 'er', or 'ir' verb.

PRACTICE A: Find the English meaning of the following verbs and conjugate them in the present tense.

1. dormir

2. costar

3. encontrar

4. Volver

5. Recorder

6. Poder

PRACTICE B: Translate the following:

1. I sleep very well in Spain.
2. Do you remember the song?
3. They return on Friday.
4. We can open the door.
5. He finds lots of things in his taxi.
6. The shoes cost 20.00 Euros

BREAK THE LANGUAGE BARRIER LEVEL 1
vickimariechats@gmail.com

DIPHTHONGS 2. The second group are verbs that change from **e** to **ie**.
E.g cerrar- to close

PERSON	TO CLOSE (INFINITIVE)	CERRAR (INFINITIVE)
1st person singular	I close	(yo) cierro
2nd person singular	You close	(tú) cierras
3rd person singular	He/she/it closes	(Él/ella) cierra
1st person plural	We close	(nosotros/as) cerramos*
2nd person plural	You (s) close	(vosotros/as) cerráis*
3rd person plural	They close	(ellos/as) cierran

PRACTICE A: Find the English meaning of the following verbs and conjugate them:

1. perder

2. comenzar

3. entender

4. preferir

5. pensar

6. querer

PRACTICE B: Translate.

1. The film starts at 9.00.
2. I don't understand Spanish verbs.
3. He prefers red wine.
4. Pedro thinks about Maria every day.
5. We always lose our sunglasses.
6. They want a house in England and they also want a house in Spain.

BREAK THE LANGUAGE BARRIER LEVEL 1
vickimariechats@gmail.com

DIPHTHONGS 3. With the third and last group of the stem-changing verbs, the **e** changes to **i**. These are only 'ir' verbs, **e.g** repetir- to repeat:

PERSON	TO REPEAT (INFINITIVE)	REPETIR (INFINITIVE)
1st person singular	I repeat	(yo) repito
2nd person singular	You repeat	(tú) repites
3rd person singular	He/she/it repeats	(Él/ella) repite
1st person plural	We repeat	(nosotros/as) repetimos*
2nd person plural	You (s) repeat	(vosotros/as) repetís*
3rd person plural	They repeat	(ellos/as) repiten

no change.

PRACTICE A: Find the English meaning of the following verbs and conjugate them.

1. Conseguir (remove the "u" in the first person singular)

2. Freir

3. Pedir

4. **Servir**

5. **Medir**

6. **Seguir** (remove the "u" in the first person singular)

PRACTICE B: Translate:

1. I fry hamburgers on Friday nights.
2. We measure the curtains.
3. The waiter serves the drinks on the terrace.
4. They always order a gin and tonic and a beer.
5. We get a job.
6. You follow the yellow car.

34. CONVERSATION PRACTICE DIPHTHONGS:

Translate these questions into Spanish and answer in Spanish using the diphthong verbs from the previous pages.

1. What do you normally order in a Chinese restaurant?
2. What time do you start work?
3. Do you sleep well in other people´s houses?
4. How much does a bottle of milk cost in Spain?
5. How do you find a good mechanic in Spain?
6. What time do you start to watch the television?
7. Do you understand a lot of Spanish?
8. Do you lose many things in the house?
9. Do you prefer red, white or rosé wine?
10. Who do you remember most from school?
11. Do you often return to your country?
12. Can you see the sea from your house?
13. Do you think that Spain is better than your country?
14. Why do you want to speak Spanish?
15. How do you get a good job in Spain?
16. What do they normally serve for breakfast in a Spanish restaurant?
17. Do you fry a lot of food?
18. Do you follow this course?

35. DIPHTHONGS - PRACTICE IN CONTEXT

PRACTICE A: Identify the 30 verbs in this text and use them to complete the verb identification table. The first 3 verbs have been done for you.

Pedro Martínez is a mechanic, and he lives in Alicante. I do not remember exactly where, but I remember that his house is near the beach. Every Friday, he goes to the bar, and he orders a menu of the day that the waiter serves on the terrace.

He returns to his house after lunch at 5, and at 8 his girlfriend Carmen arrives. They think about their future, and they count the money they have to buy a house. The house that they want costs 130 thousand euros, they have 100 thousand and they need more. They do not sleep at night because they think about how they can get enough money to buy the house.

After dinner, Pedro washes the dishes and Carmen starts to read the newspaper. They both understand that to get the money for the house, they cannot go out in the evenings.

	VERB	INFINITIVE	SPANISH	PERSON
1	is	to be	ser	3rd person singular
2	lives	to live	vivir	3rd person singular
3	do not remember	to remember	recordar (dipthong)	1st person singular
4				
5				
6				
7				
8				
9				
10				
11				
12				
13				
14				
15				
16				
17				
18				

19				
20				
21				
22				
23				
24				
25				
26				
27				
28				
29				
30				

PRACTICE B: Translate the text into Spanish.

PRACTICE C: Translate these questions into Spanish and answer them in Spanish.

1. What does Pedro do?
2. Where does he live?
3. Do I remember exactly where his house is?
4. Where does he go every Friday?
5. What does he order?
6. Where does the waiter serve the food?
7. What time does he return to his house?
8. What time does his girlfriend, Carmen, arrive?
9. What do they think about?
10. What do they count?
11. How much does the house they want cost?
12. How much do they have?
13. Why do they not sleep at night?
14. What does Pedro do after dinner?
15. What does Carmen do?
16. What do they both understand?

36. THE VERB "TENER" – TO HAVE

"**Tener**" is a very useful verb and is used for many things in Spanish besides the common meaning "**to have**". It is used often rather than the verb "**to be**" to express age and various states such as hungry, tired, thirsty etc.

Its conjugation is basically that of an "e" to "ie" dipthong, though in the first person it is a "go-go" verb. It conjugates like this:

PERSON	TO HAVE (INFINITIVE)	TENER (INFINITIVE)
1st person singular	I have	(yo) tengo
2nd person singular	You have	(tú) tienes
3rd person singular	He/she/it has	(Él/ella) tiene
1st person plural	We have	(nosotros/as) tenemos
2nd person plural	You (s) have	(vosotros/as) tenéis
3rd person plural	They have	(ellos/as) tienen

First and foremost, this is the verb we use to talk about possession, i.e what we have.

To practice, first think of 5 things you have: i.e Tengo ....
Then 5 things you dont have: i.e No tengo ....

PRACTICE A: Translate.

1. I have 10 euros.
2. You have my books.
3. She has a new car.
4. He has the cups.
5. We have a new cat.
6. You(s) have a lot of friends.
7. They have 5 cousins.
8. I don`t have the money.
9. Who has the keys?
10. Why do you have a dog in your car?
11. They have a big house in the country.
12. I have a lot of affection for him.
13. Do you(s) have any children?
14. I don´t have a present for his birthday.
15. We don´t have any pets.

AGE: In Spanish we "have" our years rather than "are" them.

Tengo 50 años- I am 50

Juan tiene 15 años- Juan is 15
La casa tiene 7 años- The house is 7 years old **¿Cuàntos años tienes?**- How old are you?

PRACTICE B: Translate the following into Spanish.

1. You are 30 years old.
2. Maria is 45 years old.
3. My car is 10 years old
4. How old is your brother?
5. Those boys are 15 years old.
6. Her cat is eight years old.
7. How old are they?
8. The town is 50 years old.

IDIOMATIC EXPRESSIONS-There are several phrases in Spanish where we use "tener" when in English we use the verb "to be".

Tener hambre-to be hungry, **Tener sed**- to be thirsty- **Tener frio**- to be cold- **Tener calor**-to be hot- **Tener miedo**- to be afraid -**Tener suerte**- to be lucky -**Tener prisa**- to be in a hurry **Tener sueño**- to be sleepy - **Tener razón**- to be right

PRACTICE C: Answer the questions appropriately in Spanish.

1. ¿Por qué comes un bocadillo?
2. ¿Por qué compra Juan una botella de agua?
3. ¿Por qué quieren dormir?
4. ¿Por qué compráis una bufanda?
5. ¿Por qué gano un millón de euros en la loteria?
6. ¿Por qué estás de acuerdo conmigo?
7. ¿Por qué corréis?
8. ¿Por qué esconden debajo de la cama?
9. ¿Por qué no estás de acuerdo con ella?
10. ¿Por qué estás sentado en la sombra?

OBLIGATION- To talk about something we "have to" do, we use the appropriate form of the verb "tener" followed by "que" followed by the infinitve of what we have to do.
E.g.- Tengo que hablar con Juan- I have to speak to Juan Tienes que comer verduras- You have to eat vegetables Tienen que trabajar mucho- They have to work hard

PRACTICE D: Think of something you have to do every day, every week, every month and every year. Then think of 5 things you don't have to do this week.

PRACTICE E : Translate the following into Spanish.

1. I have to read this book
2. You have to watch this film
3. We have to wash the car every Saturday.
4. She has to open the window every morning.
5. We have to decide now.
6. You(s) have to sell your car
7. They don't have to eat their breakfast.
8. You have to take the dog to the park.
9. We have to buy wine for the party
10. You don't have to wait here.

37. "GO-GO" VERBS

"Go-go" verbs are verbs where the first person singular ends in "go" but the other endings are regular. E.g. **salir- to leave/go out.**

PERSON	TO LEAVE/GO OUT (INFINITIVE)	SALIR (INFINITIVE)
1st person singular	I leave	(yo) sal**go**
2nd person singular	You leave	(tú) sales
3rd person singular	He/she/it leaves	(Él/ella) sale
1st person plural	We leave	(nosotros/as) salimos
2nd person plural	You (s) leave	(vosotros/as) salís
3rd person plural	They leave	(ellos/as) salen

NB: *Some "go-go" verbs are also dipthongs. For example: tener (see chapter 36.)*

PRACTICE A: Find the English meanings of the following verbs and conjugate them accordingly.

1. venir (dipthong e to ie)
2. decir (dipthong e to i)
3. hacer
4. oir (dipthong i to y)
5. poner
6. traer

PRACTICE B: Conversation Practice. Translate these questions and answer them using a "go-go" verb.

1. Do you go out much?
2. How many brothers and sisters do you have?
3. Who comes to your house on Sundays?
4. What do you hear outside your house in the morning?
5. What do you say to a Spaniard on their birthday?
6. What do you normally put on your bedside table?
7. What do you normally make for lunch on Sunday?
8. Do you have a dog?
9. What do you say when you are angry?
10. Do you come to Spain often?
11. Do you hear much Spanish where you live?
12. Where do you put your keys in the house?
13. When do you make a paella?
14. What clothes do you bring with you when you come to Spain?

38. "GUSTAR" - TO LIKE/PLEASE

The literal meaning of the verb "gustar" is "to please" rather than to like. Therefore we use only two forms, singular and plural, when we are talking about things we like.

Instead of saying "I like football", in Spanish we say "football pleases me". The person is indicated by a **PERSONAL PRONOUN**, listed below:

(me)	me	)	
(you)	te	)	gusta (singular)
(him)	le	)	
(us)	nos	)	
(yous)	os	)	gustan (plural)
(them)	les	)	

For example:

<u>Me</u> **gust**<u>a</u> el fútbol - Football pleases me / I like football
<u>Nos</u> **gust**<u>an</u> los animales - Animals please us / We like animals

*N.B: Where in English we use an "ing" word to talk about things we like "doing", for example drinking, playing, dancing, in Spanish we use the infinitive of the verb, for example to drink **(beber)** to play **(jugar)** to dance **(bailar)**. To make a negative simply put "no" first- No me gusta el futbol/ No nos gustan los animals.*

PRACTICE A: Write 5 things you like and 5 things you don´t- At least 3 plural.

PRACTICE B: Translate the following into Spanish.

1. They like to swim.
2. Do you like chocolate?
3. We like fast cars.
4. Do you(s) like reading?
5. He likes to swim.
6. I like to sing.
7. We like to go out on Saturdays.
8. She likes going out with her friends.
9. Do you like studying Spanish?
10. They like Spanish food.
11. I like cats.
12. I do not like dogs.
13. Do you not like football?
14. We do not like travelling by plane.
15. I like these shoes

PRACTICE B: GUSTAR / ENCANTAR- Find out what these activities are in English and tick the boxes for how you feel about them. Then practice saying them.

1. nadar
2. cocinar
3. los animales
4. bailar
5. beber vino
6. ir al cine
7. leer
8. trabajar
9. el chocolate
10. España
11. estudiar el español
12. ir a la playa
13. tomar el sol
14. limpiar
15. cantar karaoke
16. jugar al golf
17. hacer deporte
18. mirar la tele
19. hablar por teléfono
20. pasear

	ODIO	NO ME GUSTA NADA	NO ME GUSTA	ME GUSTA	ME GUSTA BASTANTE	ME GUSTA MUCHO	ME ENCANTA
1							
2							
3							
4							
5							
6							
7							
8							
9							
10							
11							
12							
13							
14							
15							
16							
17							
18							
19							
20							

39. "IR" - TO GO - THE HIGHLY IRREGULAR 'IR' VERB

"IR" is a very irregular verb in the present tense. It conjugates as follows:

PERSON	TO GO (INFINITIVE)	IR (INFINITIVE)
1st person singular	I go	(yo) voy
2nd person singular	You go	(tú) vas
3rd person singular	He/she/it goes	(Él/ella) va
1st person plural	We go	(nosotros/as) vamos
2nd person plural	You (s) go	(vosotros/as) vaís
3rd person plural	They go	(ellos/as) van

This verb is almost always accompanied by "a" as you are normally going "to" somewhere. For example:

Voy a la fiesta- I am going to the party.
Vamos al supermercado- We are going to the supermarket.

N.B: "a" followed by "el" contracts to "al", as "de" followed by "el" contracts to "del".

PRACTICE A: Translate the following into Spanish.

1. Where are you going?
2. They go to the beach every week.
3. We go to the bar every Sunday.
4. Where do you go on Saturdays?
5. She goes to work on the bus.
6. I go to the hospital every Tuesday morning.
7. When I need vegetables, I go to the market.
8. My brother always goes to the football.
9. To get a permit, you(s) have to go to the Town Hall.
10. When do they go to the cinema?
11. I go to Spain every year.
12. We go to their house on Mondays.
13. They go to his house on Tuesdays.
14. Do you go to the shops often?
15. Why do you not go to his house?

40. AUNT CARMEN/ TIA CARMEN

PRACTICE A: PICK OUT THE 46 VERBS IN THIS TEXT AND USE THEM TO COMPLETE THE VERB IDENTIFICATION TABLE AS PER THE EXAMPLE.

Carmen Pérez is my aunt, my mother's sister. She lives in Murcia in the South of Spain. She lives in a small, clean, and tidy flat in the City Centre. She lives alone but has a small white cat. The cat´s name is "Luna". Carmen is tall, dark and has grey eyes. She is very attractive and is thirty-five years old. She is single but has a boyfriend, Luis.

Aunt Carmen is a lawyer and has a big office near to her house. She finishes work at seven o'clock in the evening and when she arrives home, she is very tired. In her flat there are two bedrooms, one bathroom, a living room, a dining room, an office, and a kitchen.

She goes up the stairs as she doesn't like lifts and she wants to do more exercise. When she arrives at the third floor, she takes out her key, opens the door and enters. Luna always comes to say hello. She makes a lot of noise for a cat.

Carmen enters the office and turns on the computer. Then she goes into the kitchen where she makes a cup of coffee. She returns to the office and reads her emails. She sits down and starts to answer them.

Then she switches off the computer and goes to the kitchen where she prepares the dinner, then turns on the television in the living room. Her boyfriend Luis often calls her on the telephone. They chat for a short while, and then Carmen washes the dishes and decides to go to bed.

VERB IN CONTEXT	INFINITIVE	SPANISH	PERSON
1. is	To be	ser	1st p sing
2.			
3.			
4.			
5.			
6.			
7.			
8.			

#			
9.			
10.			
11.			
12.			
13.			
14.			
15.			
16.			
17.			
18.			
19.			
20.			
21.			
22.			
23.			
24.			
25.			
26.			
27.			
28.			
29.			
30.			
31.			
32.			
33.			
34.			
35.			
36.			
37.			
38.			
39.			
40.			
41.			
42.			
43.			
44.			
45.			
46.			

PRACTICE B: Translate the text into Spanish.

PRACTICE C: Translate the questions into Spanish and answer in Spanish.

1. Where does Carmen Pérez live?
2. What is her flat like and where is it?
3. Who does she live with?
4. How old is she?
5. Is she married?
6. What does she do and where does she work?
7. What time does she finish work?
8. How is she when she arrives home?
9. What is there in her flat?
10. Why does she go up the stairs?
11. What does she do when she arrives at the third floor?
12. Who comes to say "hello"?
13. What does she do in the office?
14. What does she make in the kitchen?
15. Where does she read her emails?
16. What does she do after answering them?
17. Who often calls her on the phone?
18. What does Carmen do after washing the dishes?

41. POSTSCRIPT

I hope you have enjoyed this book and that your Spanish has improved accordingly. Go over the exercises on a regular basis and practice speaking and listening as often as possible. Repetition and practice is essential for fluidity and confidence with your Spanish, but remember not to be too hard on yourself and expect immediate perfection. You will get it wrong many times before you get it right!!

Keep up the practice as much as possible. Listen to Spanish radio, watch the Spanish TV, go to the Spanish cinema, and change the language on your Netflix.

When you are confident with all the components of this Level 1 course you should be communicating effectively in Spanish and ready to move on to Level 2.

Don´t forget the YouTube channel, where you will find the audio of all the exercises. The link is below, the videos are numbered, and the page numbers are in the description. Please give a thumbs up if you find the video useful, and subscribe for updates (this is FREE, no cost involved).

You will also find all social media links and contact details.

Lastly, if you have the time and feel so inclined, please leave a review on Amazon of this book and how it has helped you to learn Spanish. Thank you ☺

Vicki

Email- vickimariechats@gmail.com

42. KEY TO "TOP TIPS".

PAGE NUMBER

1. GRAMMATICAL TERMS	7
2. ADJECTIVES	7
3. PUNCTUATION	13
4. SUBJECT PRONOUNS	13
5. POSSESIVE ADJECTIVES	13
6. APOSTROPHE PLUS "S"	28
7. "A" PLUS PROFESSION	28
8. MAKING NEGATIVES	28
9. QUESTION WORDS	41
10. ORDER OF QUESTIONS	41
11. "AL" AND "DEL"	45
12. "AT"	45
13. "TIME"- "TIEMPO", "VEZ" OR "HORA"	51
14. "HABLAR CON"	51
15. "ING" WORDS	51
16. "ON" DAYS OF THE WEEK	58
17. "PARA"- "IN ORDER TO"	58
18. THE "PERSONAL A"	58

43. ANSWERS

1. ALPHABET AND PRONUNCIATION

PRACTICE B:

- **A-** goodbye, last night, before, aeroplane
- **B-** bottle, bank, ball
- **C-**
- **D-** dolphin, inside, sport
- **E-** elephant, age, elegant
- **F-** skirt, false, date
- **G-** to catch, general, golf, goal, drop
- **H-** hospital, hotel, now
- **I-** church, English, impossible
- **J-** eye. box, to play
- **K-** kilo, kiosk, karate
- **L-** the, local, moon
- **LL-** to call, key, paella
- **M-** more, Tuesday, table
- **N-** black, cream, nothing
- **Ñ-** child/boy, morning/tomorrow, year
- **O-** other, order, eight
- **P-** bread, stick, payment
- **Q-** cheese, what/that, to want
- **R-** receipt, network/net, present
- **S-** greeting, sauce, salt
- **T-** tobacco, late/afternoon, keyboard
- **U-** one, urgent, use
- **V-** cow, ok, grape
- **W-** obvious!
- **X-** obvious!
- **Y-** yacht, plaster, I
- **Z-** shoes, light, fish

2. MASCULINE AND FEMININE

PRACTICE A:

1. La oficina
2. Un médico / una médica
3. El coche

4. Una falda
5. El aeropuerto
6. Un profesor/ una profesor
7. El perro
8. Una estrella
9. El tren
10. Un supermercado
11. El ordenador
12. Una revista
13. El restaurante
14. Una silla

PRACTICE B:

1. Las flores
2. Unas patatas
3. Las bebidas
4. Unos edificios
5. Los bancos
6. Unas tiendas
7. Las mesas
8. Unos periódicos
9. Los teléfonos
10. Unos armarios
11. Las cocinas
12. Unos jardines

4. NUMBERS PRACTICE

1. Ciento veintiuno
2. Quinientos sesenta y cinco
3. Cincuenta y cuatro
4. Mil cuatrocientos cincuenta y siete
5. Novecientos noventa y nueve
6. Seiscientos treinta y dos
7. Treinta y dos
8. Setecientos sesenta y ocho
9. Dos mil quinientos y treinta
10. Cinco mil trescientos y veinticuatro
11. Setecientos veinticuatro
12. Diecisiete
13. Ochocientos cincuenta y dos
14. Quince

15. Sesenta y uno
16. Trescientos treinta y tres
17. Mil veintitrés
18. Ciento cincuenta y cinco
19. Quinientos noventa y dos
20. Cuatrocientos treinta y uno
21. Setenta y siete
22. Ochocientos ochenta y ocho
23. Novecientos veintitrés
24. Sesenta y siete
25. Doscientos setenta y cuatro
26. Noventa y dos
27. Cinco mil doscientos treinta y dos
28. Veinticuatro
29. Ochenta y siete
30. Ciento sesenta y cinco

5. CLOTHES AND NUMBERS

PRACTICE A:

1. ¿Cuánto cuestan los guantes? - Los guantes cuestan veinticinco euros.
2. ¿Cuánto cuesta la camisa? - La camisa cuesta treinta y un euros, noventa y nueve céntimos.
3. ¿Cuánto cuesta la bufanda? - La bufanda cuesta nueve euros, noventa y nueve céntimos.
4. ¿Cuánto cuestan los pantalones? - Los pantalones cuestan quince euros, cuarenta y cuatro céntimos.
5. ¿Cuánto cuestan los zapatos? – Los zapatos cuestan dieciocho euros setenta céntimos.
6. ¿Cuánto cuestan los calcetines? - Los calcetines cuestan nueve euros, noventa y nueve céntimos.
7. ¿Cuánto cuesta el jersey? - El jersey cuesta treinta y tres euros, sesenta céntimos.
8. ¿Cuánto cuesta la falda? - La falda cuesta cuarenta y siete euros y veinte céntimos.

9. ¿Cuánto cuesta la chaqueta? - La chaqueta cuesta cuarenta y cinco euros, veinte céntimos.
10. ¿Cuánto cuesta la camiseta? - La camiseta cuesta treinta y tres euros y sesenta y dos céntimos.
11. ¿Cuánto cuesta el vestido? - El vestido cuesta noventa euros.
12. ¿Cuánto cuesta el sombrero? - El sombrero cuesta dieciocho euros, setenta y un céntimo.

6. ¿QUÉ HORA ES?

PRACTICE A:

1. Son las once y media/ Son las once y treinta.
2. Son las cuatro menos cuarto/ Son las cuatro menos quince/ Son las cuatro y cuarenta y cinco.
3. Es la una y diez.
4. Es la una menos veinticinco/ Son las doce y treinta y cinco.
5. Son las dos (en punto).
6. Son las ocho y veinticinco.
7. Son las nueve y veinte.
8. Es la una y veinticinco.
9. Son las diez y media/ Son las diez y treinta.
10. Son las nueve menos cuarto/ Son las nueve menos quince/Son las ocho y cuarenta y cinco .

7. PRACTICA LA HORA

PRACTICE A:

1. ¿A qué hora sale el tren? El tren sale a las diez y cuarto/ diez y quince
¿A qué hora llega el tren? El tren llega a las ocho (en punto)
2. ¿A qué hora sale el autobús? El autobus sale a las once y diez.
¿A qué hora llega el autobús? El autobús llega a las cinco y media/ treinta.
3. ¿A qué hora sale el avión? El avión sale a las diez y veinte.

¿A qué hora llega el avión? El avión llega a las tres y diez.
4. ¿A qué hora sale el cartero? El cartero sale a las diez y cinco.
¿A qué hora llega el cartero? El cartero llega a las tres y diez.
5. ¿A qué hora sale el médico? El médico sale a las nueve menos cuarto/ quince/ ocho y cuarenta y cinco.
¿A qué hora llega el médico? El médico llega a las diez menos cuarto/ quince/ nueve y cuarenta y cinco.
6. ¿A qué hora sale la enfermera? La enfermera sale a la una menos veinticinco/ doce y treinta y cinco.
¿A qué hora llega la enfermera? La enfermera llega a la una y cuarto/ quince.
7. ¿A qué hora sale la secretaria? La secretaria sale a las cinco menos cuarto/ quince/ cuatro y cuarenta y cinco.
¿A qué hora llega la secretaria? La secretaria llega a las dos y media/ treinta.
8. ¿A qué hora sale la señora? La señora sale a las seis menos diez/ cinco y cincuenta.
¿A qué hora llega la señora? La señora llega a las siete menos veinte/ seis y cuarenta.
9. ¿A qué hora sale la profesora? La profesora sale a las tres y veinticinco.
¿A qué hora llega la profesora? La profesora llega a las once y veinticinco.
10. ¿A qué hora sale María? María sale a la una y veinte.
¿A qué hora llega María? María llega a las seis y cinco.

PRACTICE B:

1. ¿A qué hora comienza el partido? El partido comienza a las diez y cuarto/

quince.
¿A qué hora termina el partido? El partido termina a las doce y cuarto/ quince.

2. ¿A qué hora comienza el programa? El programa comienza a las cuatro y cuarto/ quince.
¿A qué hora termina el programa? El programa termina a las cinco y Media/ treinta.

3. ¿A qué hora comienza el espectáculo? El espectáculo comienza a las diez y veinte.
¿A qué hora termina el espectáculo? El espectáculo termina a las tres y diez.

4. ¿A qué hora comienza la feria? La feria comienza a las nueve y veinte.
¿A qué hora termina la feria? La feria termina a las ocho menos veinte/ siete y cuarenta.

5. ¿A qué hora comienza el cantante? El cantante comienza a las nueve menos cuarto/ quince.
¿A qué hora termina el cantante? El cantante termina a las diez menos cuarto/ quince.

6. ¿A qué hora comienza la comida? La comida comienza a la una y media/ treinta.
¿A qué hora termina la comida? La comida termina a las cuatro menos diez/ tres y cincuenta.

7. ¿A qué hora comienza la fiesta? La fiesta comienza a las cinco menos cuarto/ quince/ cuatro y cuarenta y cinco.
¿A qué hora termina la fiesta? La fiesta termina a las dos y media.

8. ¿A qué hora comienza la cena? La cena comienza a las diez y diez.
¿A qué hora termina la cena? La cena termina a la una y cuarto.

9. ¿A qué hora comienza la clase? La clase comienza a las tres y veinticinco.

¿A qué hora termina la clase? La clase termina a las once y cinco.
10. ¿A qué hora comienza el baile? El baile comienza a las once y media
/treinta.
¿A qué hora termina el baile? El baile termina a las cuatro (en punto).

8. THE FIRST VERB "TO BE" – "SER"

PRACTICE B:

1. (Nosotros) somos ingleses.
2. La mesa es cuadrada.
3. ¿Eres (tú) médico?
4. ¿Sois (vosotros) profesores?
5. (Ella) es alta.
6. (Ellos) son de España.
7. (Yo) soy Juan.
8. (Él) es camarero.
9. (Yo) soy de los Estados Unidos.
10. (Vosotros) sois mis amigos.
11. (Él) es guapo.
12. (Ella) es muy intresante.
13. (Ellos) son franceses de Paris.
14. (Vosotros) sois profesores.
15. Hoy es martes.
16. Mis calcetines son blancos.
17. ¿Quién eres (tú)?
18. Jennifer Aniston es actríz.

9. DESCRIPTIONS - Masculine and Feminine Adjectives

PRACTICE A:

1. Los restaurants son muy baratos en España.
2. El vino es muy caro en Inglaterra.
3. La casa es grande.
4. Peter y Mary son ingleses.
5. Carmen y María son españolas.
6. Ellos son altos.
7. El coche es pequeño.
8. La lámpara es blanca.

9. La falda es demasiada pequeña.
10. El pasillo es estrecho.
11. La cocina es ancha.
12. Español es facíl.
13. (Tú) eres famoso.
14. (Ella) es famosa.
15. (Nosotros) somos padres.

10. THE VERB "SER" IN CONTEXT

PRACTICE B: Verbs

1. Soy
2. soy
3. soy
4. eres
5. Soy
6. Son
7. son
8. es
9. es
10. es
11. es
12. es
13. Es
14. Es
15. Es
16. Es

TRANSLATION

Klaus: Hello, I´m Klaus
Janet: I´m Janet
Klaus: Pleased to meet you. I´m German, from Munich. And you Janet? Where are you from?
Janet: I´m English, from London.
Klaus: Are they also English?
Janet: No, they are not English. Paulo is Italian, from Rome. Claudia is French, from Paris. Frank is American, from New York.
Who is the Spanish teacher?
Klaus: Pedro Pérez is the teacher.
Janet: What is Pedro Pérez like?
Klaus: He is tall, dark, and very nice.
Janet: Is he Spanish or Argentinian?
Klaus: He´s Spanish, from Madrid.

PRACTICE C:

1. ¿De dónde es Klaus? Klaus es alemán, de Múnich.
2. ¿De dónde es Janet? Janet es inglesa, de Londrés
3. ¿Es Paulo italiano? Si, Paulo es italiano, de Roma.
4. ¿Es Claudia alemana? No. Claudia no es alemana. Claudia es francesa, de Paris.
5. ¿De dónde es Frank? Frank es americano, de Nueva York.
6. ¿Quién es el professor? Pedro Pérez es el profesor.
7. ¿Qué es Pedro Pérez? Pedro Pérez es el profesor.
8. ¿Cómo es Pedro Pérez? Es alto, moreno y muy simpático.
9. ¿De dónde es Pedro Pérez? Es español, de Madrid.
10. ¿De dónde eres (tú)? Free answer

PRACTICE D:

JOHN: Hola, soy Juan. ¿Quién eres?
MARIA: Soy María. ¿Eres estudiante de español?
JOHN: No, no soy estudiante de español, soy estudiante de alemán. ¿Y tú?
MARIA: Soy estudiante de alemán también.
JOHN: ¿De dónde eres?
MARIA: Soy española, de Alicante. ¿Y tú?
JOHN: Soy inglés, de Manchester.
MARIA: ¿Quién es el profesor de alemán?
JOHN: Señora Schmidt.
MARIA: ¿Cómo es?
JOHN: Es baja, rubia, y muy simpática.

PRACTICE E:

1. ¿Es John estudiante de español? No, no es estudiante de español, es estudiante de alemán.
2. ¿Es María estudiante de español? No, no es estudiante de español, es estudiante de alemán también.
3. ¿De dónde es María? María es española, de Alicante.
4. ¿De dónde es John? John es inglés, de Manchester.
5. ¿Quién es el profesor de alemán? Señora Schmidt es la profesora de

alemán.
6. ¿Cómo es Señora Schmidt? Es baja, rubia, y muy simpática.
7. ¿Quién es tu profesor/a de español? Free answer
8. ¿Cómo es? Free answer
9. ¿De dónde eres (tú)? Free answer
10. ¿Cómo eres (tú?) Free answer

11. CONVERSATION PRACTICE "SER"

1. ¿De dónde eres?
2. ¿Cómo es tu coche?
3. ¿Cuál día es hoy?
4. ¿Qué hora es?
5. ¿Cuándo es tu cumpleaños
6. ¿Qué/ cuál es tu comida preferida/ favorita
7. ¿Quién es tu actor favorito/a/ preferido/ a?
8. ¿De qué color es tu casa?
9. ¿Por qué es español necesario?
10. ¿Cuándo es la clase de español?
11. ¿Quién es tu mejor amigo/ amigo mejor?
12. ¿Cómo eres?

FREE ANSWERS

12. THE SECOND VERB "TO BE" - "ESTAR"

PRACTICE B:

1. Estoy con mi marido.
2. No estoy con mi marido.
3. Estamos cansados.
4. Estáis contentos.
5. Están tristes.
6. Pedro y Carmen están en Madrid.
7. Estoy triste porque no estás aqui.
8. ¿Por qué no estás felíz/contento?
9. ¿Está casado o soltero?
10. Ella está en clase y él está en la oficina.
11. Los perros están el el jardín.
12. Estamos enfadados.
13. El cielo está gris.
14. Begoña está divorciada.
15. El café está frio.
16. ¿Cómo estás?
17. ¿Cómo está tu amigo Miguel?

18. ¿Dónde está la Comisaria?
19. ¿Dónde están los sobres?
20. ¿Cómo estáis?
21. Estás muy inquieto.
22. María está enferma.
23. Juan está casado.
24. Los dos niños están en el jardín.
25. El teléfono está en/sobre/encima de la mesa.
26. Las manzanas están el la bolsa.
27. La cocina está limpia.
28. ¿Está abierto el bar?
29. Todas las ventanas y puertas están cerradas.
30. Los libros están en el sofá.

13. DESCRIPTIONS- "ESTAR"

1. Las puertas y ventanas están abiertas.
2. El suelo en su casa nunca está sucio.
3. La gente está muy enfadada.
4. Estamos muy tristes porque están enfermos.
5. Por fin, la cocina está limpia.
6. Siempre estáis contentos/ felices los viernes.
7. Pedro está casado pero Carmen está divorciada.
8. La silla está libre en este momento.
9. Estoy más cómodo/a en mis zapatos viejos/ antiguos.
10. No están comódos con la situación.
11. ¿Estás enfermo?
12. María está resfriado pero Paco está bien.
13. Maite y Dulce están las dos/ ambas muy contentas con su trabajo.
14. No estamos cómodos hoy porque tenemos frio.
15. Están enfadados con nosotros hoy.

14. THE VERB "ESTAR" IN CONTEXT - EN LA CLASE

PRACTICE B: Verbs

16. estás
17. Estoy
18. Estoy

12. Estoy
13. estoy
14. Es

4.	está	15.	está
5.	está	16.	Está
6.	está	17.	estoy
7.	Está	18.	está
8.	Está	19.	está
9.	está	20.	Estás
10.	Está	21.	estoy
11.	estás		

PRACTICE C:

Pablo: Good day, Carmen. How are you?
Carmen: I am very well thank you. And you?
Pablo: I am very well also. Where is your sister María?
Carmen: She is not in class today. She is at home.
Pablo: Why? Is she ill?
Carmen: Yes, she has a cold.
Pablo: Where is the house?
Carmen : In San Juan Street, number 18, on the left of the street.
Pablo : Thanks.
(In Maria´s house)
Pablo : Hi Maria, how are you?
María :I have a cold, but today I am a little better.
Pablo :I like your house, it is very nice/ pretty.
María : Yes, but today it is very untidy. Is the door open? I am cold, I am not comfortable.
Pablo : Yes, the door is open. Now it is closed. Are you comfortable now?
María :   Yes, now I am fine.

PRACTICE D:

1. ¿Cómo está Carmen? Carmen está muy bien.
2. ¿Dónde está su hermana María? Su hermana María está en casa.
3. ¿Está enferma? Si, está resfriada.
4. ¿Dónde está la casa? (La casa) está en Calle San Juan, número 18, a la izquierda de la calle.
5. ¿Cómo está María? Está resfriada, pero hoy está un poco mejor.
6. ¿Cómo es la casa? La casa es muy bonita.
7. ¿Cómo está hoy? Hoy está muy desordenada.
8. ¿Está cómoda María? No, no está cómoda. (Tiene frio)

9. ¿Por qué tiene frio? La puerta está abierta. (See chapter 24.)
10. ¿Está comodá ahora? Si, ahora está cómoda.
11. ¿Cómo estás (tú) hoy? Free answer.
12. ¿Estás cómodo/a? Free answer.

15. TRANSLATION "ESTAR"

IN THE CLASS

PRACTICE A:

Pedro: Buenos días Pablo, ¿Cómo estás? Pablo: Estoy muy bien gracias. ¿Y tú?
Pedro: Estoy enfermo. Estoy resfriado.
Pablo: ¿Por qué no estás en la casa? ¿Dónde está tu casa?
Pedro: Tengo una clase de inglés. Mi casa está en Calle Cartagena, número trece, a la derecha.
Pablo: Tengo una clase de inglés también. Me gusta la clase mucho es muy interesante.
Pedro: Sí, pero cuando la ventana está abierta tengo frio. Pablo: Está cerrada hoy. ¿Estás cómodo?
Pedro: Sí, estoy muy cómodo gracias. ¿Y tú? Pablo: Sí. Yo también.

PRACTICE B:

1. ¿Cómo está Pedro?
2. ¿Por qué no está en la casa?
3. ¿Cómo está Pablo?
4. ¿Dónde está la casa de Pedro?
5. ¿Cómo es la clase?
6. ¿Está la ventana abierta o cerrada?
7. ¿Cómo estás (tú) hoy?
8. ¿Estás cómodo/a?

16. CONVERSATION PRACTICE "ESTAR"

1. ¿Dónde estás?
2. ¿Estás casado?
3. ¿Dónde está Barcelona?
4. ¿Estás cansado/a?
5. ¿Estás felíz/ content/a?

6. ¿Qué color está el cielo hoy?
7. ¿Cómo estás?
8. ¿Estás enfermo/a?
9. ¿Dónde está el Palacio de Buckingham?
10. ¿Dónde está la clase de español?
11. ¿Cuándo estás triste?
12. ¿Cuándo estás felíz/ content/a?

FREE ANSWERS

18. SER AND ESTAR - CONVERSATION PRACTICE

1. ¿De dónde eres?
2. ¿Dónde está tu casa?
3. ¿Cómo es tu casa?
4. ¿Cuándo es Navidad?
5. ¿Dónde está Madrid?
6. ¿Por qué es importante el español para tí?
7. ¿Cómo es España?
8. ¿Quién es tu mejor amigo?
9. ¿Dónde está tu coche?
10. ¿Cuándo es tu cumpleaños?
11. ¿Estás cansado?
12. ¿Estás contento/a?
13. ¿De qué color es tu coche?
14. ¿Cuál/ Qué día es?
15. ¿Con quíen estás?
16. ¿Cuál es mejor, España o Gran Bretaña?
17. ¿Estás en casa?
18. ¿Cuándo es la clase de español?
19. ¿Quién es el Presidente de España?
20. ¿Está el cielo gris hoy?

FREE ANSWERS

19. HAY

PRACTICE A: (free answers)

1. ¿Cuántos dormitorios hay en tu casa?
2. ¿Hay una televisión en tu dormitorio?
3. ¿Hay flores en tu jardín?
4. ¿Hay cuadros en tu salón?
5. ¿Hay animales en tu casa?
6. ¿Cuántos árboles hay en tu jardín?
7. ¿Hay buenos restaurantes cerca de tu casa?

8. ¿Hay muchos libros en tu casa?
9. ¿Hay un coche delante de tu casa?
10. ¿Qué hay en tu mesita de noche?

20. HAY/ ESTAR/ SER

PRACTICE B:

11. HAY ...

A table	A magazine
A chair	A newspaper
A window	A television
A picture	A book
A lamp	A light
A radio	A sofa
A rug	A bookcase
An armchair	A wardrobe

12.   ESTÁ / ESTÁN ...

On the right/left	In the centre of
On/above	In the corner
On/in	Around
On top of	Under
In front of	Between
Behind	On the wall
At the side of/next to	Near to

13.   ES / SON ...

High	Square
Low	Big
Long	Small
Rectangular	Round
Narrow	Wide

PRACTICE C: (free answers)

22. ¿QUIÉN ES?/ ¿QUIENES SON? – Who is it?/ Who are they?

PRACTICE A: Translate into English and guess who it is.

1. He is a billionaire. He is American. He has short, brown hair. He is quite tall with brown eyes. He is a businessperson and the owner of Twitter. He is more or less 55 years old and is three times

divorced. **ELON MUSK**

2. He is American. He is dead. He is black with long curly hair. He is very slim and is a singer and dances very well. He has 4 adopted children. He is 50. He has a lot of siblings. Whos is he? **MICHAEL JACKSON**

3. He is English. He is not very tall. He is nearly bald and has big ears. He has blue eyes. He is very rich. He has married and has 2 sons. His family is royal. He wears a crown. He is more or less 75 years old. He talks to plants and trees and his sons are Princes. Who is he? **PRINCE CHARLES**

PRACTICE D:

1. She is American. She is dark with short hair and brown eyes. She is more or less 60 years old. She is very tall, slim and attractive. She is married to a very famous politician. She has 2 daughters. Who is she? **MICHELE OBAMA**

2. She is American, attractive and dark with long straight hair. She is divorced from a very famous American actor and they have a lot of adopted children. Her father is also a famous actor, John Voight. She is more or less 50 years old. She is famous for her large lips. Who is she? **ANGELINA JOLIE**

3. She is American, she is thirty-five years old. She is blonde, slim and attractive. She is an actor and a Singer. She is divorced and has no children. She sings "Happy Birthday" to the President. She is dead. Who is she? **MARILYN MONROE**

PRACTICE F:

1. They are actors. They are not attractive. One is tall, slim and blonde. The other is also tall, but fat and bald. He is Amertican. They are comics. They always wear suits and black hats. Their films are in black and white. Who are they? **LAUREL AND HARDY**

2. They Are married. They are English. He is tall, attractive and slim. He has very short blonde hair. She is short, very slim, darkwith dark hair. She is very attractive. He is a footballer and she is a businesswoman now, before a singer. They have 4

choildren. They are more or less 50 years old. Who are they?
THE BECKHAMS

3. They are married and have two children. He is English and she is American. She is an actor, he is from royal family. They are more or less 35 years old. They live in the United States. He is a redhead with blue eyes and she is dark with brown eyes. They are both attractive. Who are they? **HARRY AND MEGHAN**

23 LA CASA DE PEDRO

PRACTICE B: Verbs

1. es
2. es
3. es
4. está
5. está
6. está
7. es
8. es
9. está
10. está
11. es
12. está
13. está

PRACTICE C:

Pedro Martínez is Spanish. He is from Alicante. He is a mechanic. Where is he today? Today he is in the house/at home. In the house there are two bedrooms, a bathroom, a kitchen, a dining room and a living room. Pedro is in the living room. What is the living room like? It is very big. In the living room there is a table, a sofa, an armchair, some chairs and a telvision. On the floor there is a rug. A dog is sitting on the rug under a chair. Pedro´s mother is sitting in the armchair. The armchair is very comfortable. Pedro is sitting on the sofa. What is there on the table? On the table there is a cup and in the cup there is coffee. Also there is a magazine and some books. On the wall there is a mirror and some pictures. The television is under the clock.

PRACTICE D:

1. ¿De dónde es Pedro? Pedro es español de Alicante.
2. ¿Qué es Pedro? Pedro es mecánico.
3. ¿Dónde está hoy? Hoy está en casa.
4. ¿Cuántos dormitorios hay en la casa? Hay 2 dormitorios en la casa
5. ¿Cómo es la sala? La sala es muy grande.
6. ¿Qué hay en el suelo? Sobre el suelo hay una alfombra.
7. ¿Dónde está la madre de Pedro? La

madre de Pedro está sentada en el sillón.
8. ¿Qué hay sobre/en la mesa? Sobre la mesa hay una taza (y en la taza hay café.)
9. ¿Dónde están los cuadros? Los cuadros están en la pared.
10. ¿Dónde está la televisión? La televisión está debajo del espejo.

24. REGULAR VERBS - 1ST CONJUGATION – 'AR' VERBS

PRACTICE A:

1. to walk - ando, andas, anda, andamos, andáis, andan.
2. to dance - bailo, bailas. baila, bailamos, bailáis, bailan.
3. to look for - busco, buscas, busca, buscamos, buscáis, buscan.
4. to sing - canto, cantas, canta, cantamos, cantáis, cantan.
5. to study - estudio, estudias, estudia, estudiamos, estudiáis, estudian.
6. to buy - compro, compras, compra, compramos, compráis, compran
7. ¿Adónde andamos?
8. ¿Cuándo bailas?
9. ¿Qué busca?
10. ¿Dónde estudiáis español?
11. ¿Dónde compras la carne?
12. ¿Cuándo escucha la radio?
13. ¿Cuándo llegan?
14. ¿Qué espero?
15. ¿Qué miras?

PRACTICE D: (free answers)

1. ¿Qué idiomas hablas?
2. ¿Cuándo bailas?
3. ¿Cantas en karaoke?
4. ¿Dónde estudias español?
5. ¿Cuándo practicas español?
6. ¿Dónde trabajas?
7. ¿Cómo preparas una tortilla?
8. ¿Qué música escuchas en la radio?

9. ¿Dónde compras la ropa?
10. ¿Buscas nuevo coche?
11. ¿Qué llevas?
12. ¿Andas al trabajo?
13. ¿Qué instrumentas tocas?
14. ¿Cuándo miras la televisión?

25. 'AR' VERBS IN CONTEXT

PRACTICE A: verbs

VERB IN CONTEXT	INFINITIVE	ENGLISH	PERSON
1. son	ser	To be	3rd p plural
2. están	estar	To be	3rd p.plural
3. están	estar	To be	3rd p.plural
4. estudia	estudiar	To study	3rd p. singular
5. estudia	estudiar	To study	3rd p. singular
6. estudian	estudiar	To study	3rd p.plural
7. son	ser	To be	3rd p.plural
8. habla	hablar	To speak	3rd p. singular
9. habla	hablar	To speak	3rd p. singular
10. practica	practicar	To practice	3rd p. singular
11. habla	hablar	To speak	3rd p. singular
12. habla	hablar	To speak	3rd p. singular
13. practica	practicar	To practice	3rd p. singular
14. trabajan	trabajar	To work	3rd p.plural
15. trabaja	trabajar	To work	3rd p. singular
16. trabaja	trabajar	To work	3rd p. singular
17. ganan	ganar	To earn	3rd p. plural
18. comprar	comprar	To buy	infinitive
19. pagar	pagar	To pay	infinitive
20. andan	andar	To walk	3rd p.plural
21. está	estar	To be	3rd p. singular
22. estudian	estudiar	To study	3rd p.plural
23. practican	practicar	To practice	3rd p.plural
24. miran	mirar	To watch	3rd p.plural
25. prepara	preparar	To prepare	3rd p. singular
26. toca	tocar	To play	3rd p. singular
27. cenar	cenar	To dine	infinitive
28. escuchan	escuchar	To listen	3rd p.plural
29. hablan	hablar	To speak	3rd p.plural
30. practicar	practicar	To practice	infinitive

PRACTICE B:

BREAK THE LANGUAGE BARRIER LEVEL 1
vickimariechats@gmail.com

Pedro and María are Spanish but now they are in England. They are at Manchester University. Pedro studies English and María studies English also. They study a lot and they are very good students.

María speaks English perfectly, and she also speaks French, Spanish and a little German. She practises every day at the University and with her friends. Pedro speaks English perfectly too, but he doesn´t speak French or German. He practices a lot with the other students and his friends.

On Saturdays, they both work. Pedro works in an office and María works in a shop. They earn money to buy clothes and pay the rent. Every day they walk to the University. Their house is very close.

In the evenings, after classes, they study a little, they practice English with their friends, and later they watch TV at home. Pedro prepares the dinner and María plays the guitar. After dinner, they listen to the radio, and speak only in English to practice more.

PRACTICE C:

1. ¿De dónde son Pedro y María? Pedro y María son de España.
2. ¿Dónde están ahora? Ahora están en Inglaterra.
3. ¿Qué estudia Pedro? Pedro estudia inglés.
4. ¿Quién estudia ingles también? María estudia inglés tambíen.
5. ¿Qué idiomas habla María también? María habla francés, español y un poco de alemán también.
6. ¿Cuándo practica? Practica todos los días en la Universidad y con los amigos.
7. ¿Trabajan los dos? Sí, Los dos trabajan.
8. ¿Quién trabaja en una tienda? María trabaja en una tienda.
9. ¿Por qué ganan dinero? Ganan dinero para comprar ropa y comida y pagar el alquiler.
10. ¿Cómo llegan a la Universidad? Todos los días andan a la Universidad.
11. ¿Cuándo miran la tele? Miran la tele por la tarde.

12. ¿Quién prepara la cena? Pedro prepara la cena.
13. ¿Qué instrumento toca María? María toca la guitarra.
14. ¿Por qué hablan solamente en inglés? Hablan solamente en inglés para practicar más.

26. REGULAR VERBS - 2ᴺᴰ CONJUGATION - 'ER' VERBS

PRACTICE A:

1. beber - to drink - bebo, bebes, bebe, bebemos, bebéis, beben.
2. aprender - to learn - aprendo, aprendes, aprende, aprendemos, aprendéis, aprenden.
3. creer - to think or to believe - creo, crees, cree, creemos, creéis, creen.
4. vender - to sell - vendo, vendes, vende, vendemos, vendéis, venden.
5. leer - to read - leo, lees, lee, leemos, leéis, leen.
6. comprender - to understand - comprendo, comprendes, comprende, comprendemos, comprendéis, comprenden.
7. correr - to run - corro, corres, corre, corremos, corréis, corren.
8. deber - to "must"/to owe - debo, debes, debe, debemos, debéis, deben.
9. romper - to break - rompo, rompes, rompe, rompemos, rompéis, rompen
10. ver - to see/to watch - veo, ves, ve, vemos, véis, ven.

PRACTICE B:

1. A menudo como en un restaurante español.
2. Bebo leche todos los días.
3. No comprendo ruso.
4. Leo muchos libros.
5. Aprendo mucho español en el Internet.
6. Manuel vende ropa en el mercadillo.
7. Carmen siempre corre en el maratón.

8. Creemos en los OVNIs.
9. Muchos americanos comprenden español.
10. Deben aprender español.
11. Rompo algo todos los días.
12. Ve la tele los fines de semana.
13. Siempre bebe cerveza en el bar.
14. Debemos comer más verduras.
15. Normalmente venden coches pero en verano venden casas.

PRACTICE C: (free answers)

1. ¿Qué ves de la ventana de tu dormitorio?
2. ¿Por qué debes estudiar español?
3. ¿Comprendes los verbos españoles?
4. ¿Qué bebes en un restaurante?
5. ¿Crees en los fantasmas?
6. ¿Vendes tu casa?
7. ¿Rompes muchas cosas?
8. ¿Lees muchos libros?
9. ¿Dónde normalmente comes los domingos?
10. ¿Comes verduras?
11. ¿Cuándo bebes alcohol en la casa?
12. ¿Cuándo corres?
13. ¿Por qué estudias español?
14. ¿Por qué debes beber agua en verano?
15.

27. 'ER' VERBS IN CONTEXT

PRACTICE A: *verb table*

VERB	INFINITIVE	ENGLISH	PERSON
1. están	estar	To be	3rd p. plural
2. bebe	beber	To drink	3rd p.singular
3. bebe	beber	To drink	3rd p.singular
4. lee	leer	To read	3rd p.singular
5. lee	leer	To read	3rd p.singular
6. comprenden	comprender	To understand	3rd p.plural
7. aprenden	aprender	To learn	3rd p.plural
8. aprenden	aprender	To learn	3rd p.plural
9. leen	leer	To read	3rd p.plural
10. ven	ver	To watch/see	3rd p.plural
11. creen	creer	To believe	3rd p.plural
12. es	ser	To be	3rd p.singular
13. ve	ver	To see/watch	3rd p.singular
14. vende	vender	To sell	3rd p.singular

15.creen	creer	To think/believe	3rd p.plural
16.deben	deber	To must	3rd p.plural
17.comprar	comprar	To buy	infinitive
18.hacer	hacer	To do/make	infinitive
19.comen	comer	To eat/have lunch	3rd p.plural
20.come	comer	To eat/have lunch	3rd p.singular
21. come	comer	To eat/have lunch	3rd p.singular
22. come	comer	To eat/have lunch	3rd p.singular
23. come	comer	To eat/have lunch	3rd p.singular
24. comer	comer	To eat/have lunch	infinitive
25.beben	beber	To drink	3rd p.plural
26.terminan	terminar	To finish	3rd p.plural
27.comer	comer	To eat/have lunch	infinitive
28.pagan	pagar	To pay	3rd p.plural
29.rompe	romper	To break	3rd p. singular

30.está	estar	To be	3rd p.singular
31.está	estar	To be	3rd p.singular
32.corren	correr	To run	3rd p.plural
33.es	ser	To be	3rd p.singular
34.deben	deber	To must	3rd p.plural
35.coger	coger	To get/catch	3rd p.plural

Translation

Pedro and María are in a restaurant in the centre of the City of Manchester. María drinks/is drinking red wine and Pedro drinks/is drinking beer. María reads/is reading a magazine and Pedro reads/is reading a newspaper. They understand a lot of the words in English, but not all of them. They learn a lot of English with their English friends, but they also learn a lot when they read newspapers and magazines, and when they watch television at night. They think that English is very important for their future. Pedro sees an advert in the newspaper, a boy is selling a bicycle. They both believe that they should buy this bicycle to do more exercise.

For starter, they both eat salad. For main course, María eats paella and Pedro eats macarrones. For dessert, Pedro eats flan and María eats rice pudding. After lunch, they both drink white coffee.

They finish eating at around four o'clock. When they pay the bill, Pedro breaks a glass that is on the table. The waiter is not angry, and they both run to the bus stop because now it is late, and they must catch the bus at a quarter past four.

PRACTICE B:

1. ¿Dónde están Pedro y María? - Pedro y María están en un restaurante español en el centro de la ciudad de Manchester.
2. ¿Qué bebe María? - María bebe vino tinto.
3. ¿Quién bebe cerveza? - Pedro bebe cerveza.
4. ¿Qué leen? - María lee una revista y Pedro lee un periódico.
5. ¿Cuándo aprenden mucho inglés? - Aprenden mucho inglés con sus amigos ingleses, pero también aprenden mucho cuando leen periódicos y revistas, y cuando ven la tele por la noche.
6. ¿Por qué creen que el inglés es muy importante? - Creen que el inglés es muy importante para su futuro.
7. ¿Qué ve Pedro en el periódico? - Pedro ve un anuncio en el periódico.
8. ¿Qué vende el chico? – El chico vende una bicicleta. ¿Por qué creen que deben comprar esta bicicleta? Creen que deben comprar esta bicicleta para hacer más ejercicio.
9. ¿Qué comen los dos de primero? - De primero, los dos comen ensalada.
10. ¿Quién come paella de segundo? - María come paella de segundo.
11. ¿Qué come Pedro de postre? - Pedro come flan de postre.
12. ¿Qué beben los dos después de comer? - Después de comer, los dos beben café con leche.
13. ¿A qué hora terminan de comer? Terminan de comer a las cuatro más o menos.
14. ¿Qué rompe Pedro cuándo pagan la cuenta? - Cuando pagan la cuenta, Pedro rompe un vaso que está en la mesa.
15. ¿Está enfadado el camarero? – No, el camarero no está enfadado.

16. ¿Por qué corren a la parada del autobús? - Corren a la parada del autobús porque ahora es tarde.
17. ¿A qué hora deben coger el autobús? - Deben coger el autobús a las cuatro y cuarto.

28. REGULAR VERBS - 3ʳᵈ CONJUGATION – 'IR' VERBS

PRACTICE A:

1. escribir - to write - escribo, escribes, escribe, escribimos, escribís, escriben.
2. recibir - to receive - recibo, recibes, recibe, recibimos, recibís, reciben.
3. cubrir - to cover - cubro, cubres, cubre, cubrimos, cubrís, cubren.
4. subir - to go up/to get on/to climb - subo, subes, sube, subimos, subís, suben.
5. descubrir – to discover - descubro, descubres, descubre, descubrimos, descubrís, descubren.
6. compartir – to share - comparto, compartes, comparte, compartimos, compartís, comparten.
7. sufrir – to suffer - sufro, sufres, sufre, sufrimos, sufrís, sufren
8. repartir - to hand out - reparto, repartes, reparte, repartimos, repartís, reparten.
9. abrir – to open - abro, abres, abre, abrimos, abrís, abren.
10. discutir – to discuss/to argue - discuto, discutes, discute, discutimos, discutís, discuten.

PRACTICE B:

1. ¿Escribes muchos emails?
2. En África, muchos niños sufren.
3. La nieve cubre las montañas.
4. Subo el tren en Barcelona.
5. Siempre descubrimos la verdad al final.
6. El profesor reparte los exámenes.
7. Juan and Pedro comparten un piso en Madrid.
8. ¿Recibís muchas cartas?
9. Siempre abre la puerta para mí.
10. Discuten cada sábado por la noche.

29. TRANSLATION FROM ENGLISH TO SPANISH - REGULAR VERBS

PRACTICE A: verbs

1. lives
2. works
3. studies
4. watches
5. speaks
6. He doesn't understand
7. reads
8. visits
9. drinks
10. eats
11. sells
12. writes
13. learns
14. is
15. has
16. is
17. shares

PRACTICE B:

Marcos vive en Bendiorm con su familia. Trabaja en un banco, y los miércoles por la tarde estudia inglés en una escuela privada. Mira/ve la tele los lunes, y los martes habla con sus amigos ingleses. No comprende todo.
Los jueves lee libros de historia, y los viernes visita un bar local. Siempre bebe vino tinto y come tapas. Los sábados vende pollos en el mercadillo, y los domingos escribe emails a sus amigos en Inglaterra. Aprende mucho inglés con ellos.

Marcos es alto, moreno, y tiene ojos castaños. Es muy simpático y comparte todo con su familia.

PRACTICE C:

1. ¿Dónde vive Marcos y con quién?
   Marcos vive en Benidorm con su Familia.
2. ¿Dónde trababja? Trabaja en un banco.

3. ¿Qué estudia los miércoles por la tarde? Los miércoles por la tarde estudia inglés.
4. ¿Dónde estudia? Estudia en una escuela privada.
5. ¿Qué hace los lunes? Los lunes mira/ve la tele.
6. ¿Con quién habla los martes? Los martes habla con sus amigos ingleses.
7. ¿Comprende todo? No, no comprende todo.
8. ¿Qué lee los los jueves? Los jueves lee libros de historia.
9. ¿Qué siempre come y bebe en su bar local los viernes? Siempre bebe vino tinto y come tapas en su bar local.
10. ¿Qué vende en el mercadillo los sábados? Los sábados vende pollos en el mercadillo.
11. ¿A quién escribe los domingos? Escribe emails a sus amigos en Inglaterra los domingos.
12. ¿Cómo es Marcos? Marcos es alto, moreno, y tiene ojos castaños. Es muy simpático y comparte todo con su familia.

30. ADVERBS OF FREQUENCY

PRACTICE A:

1. siempre
2. a menudo
3. por lo general/normalmente
4. a veces
5. casi nunca
6. nunca
7. de vez en cuando
8. una vez por/ a la semana
9. una vez por/ al mes
10. una vez por/al año
11. cada día/todos los días
12. cada semana/todas las semanas
13. cada mes/ todos los meses
14. cada sábado/ todos los sábados
15. cada mañana/todas las mañanas
16. cada tarde/ todas las tardes

PRACTICE B: *(free answers)*

CONVERSATION PRACTICE REGULAR VERBS

1. ¿Qué idiomas hablas?
2. ¿Dónde vives?
3. ¿Cuándo bailas?
4. ¿Abres la ventana en tu dormitorio por la noche?
5. ¿Qué bebes en un retaurante?
6. ¿Crees en los fantasmas?
7. ¿Cantas en karaoke?
8. ¿Cuándo practicas español?
9. ¿Dónde trabajas?
10. ¿Cuándo bebes alcohol en la casa?
11. ¿Cuándo corres?
12. ¿Qué música escuchas en la radio?
13. ¿Dónde compras la ropa?
14. ¿Recibes muchas cartas?
15. ¿Rompes muchas cosas?
16. ¿Lees muchos libros?
17. ¿Qué llevas?
18. ¿Andas cada día/ todos los días?
19. ¿Qué instrumentos tocas?
20. ¿Cuándo miras/ ves la tele/ televisión?
21. ¿Dónde hablas español?
22. ¿Por qué debes estudiar español?
23. ¿Andas a la playa?
24. ¿Comprendes verbos españoles?

(free answers)

32. PRACTICE OF REGULAR VERBS

PRACTICE B:

	VERB IN CONTEXT	INFINITIVE	ENGLISH	MEANING IN CONTEXT	PERSON
1	es	ser	to be	is	3rd person singular
2	vivimos	vivir	to live	we live	1st person plural
3	trabaja	trabajar	to work	he works	3rd person singular
4	trabaja	trabajar	to work	she works	3rd person singular
5	trabajan	trabajar	to work	they work	3rd person plural
6	sale	salir	to leave	he leaves	3rd person singular
7	coge	coger	to catch	he catches	3rd person sing

BREAK THE LANGUAGE BARRIER LEVEL 1
vickimariechats@gmail.com

8	coge	coger	to catch	she catches	3rd person singular
9	estudio	estudiar	to study	I study	1st person singular
10	regreso	regresar	to return	I return	1st person singular
11	como	comer	to eat/have lunch	I eat/have lunch	1st person singular
12	comen	comer	to eat/have lunch	hey eat/have lunch	3rd person plural
13	trabaja	trabajar	to work	she works	3rd person singular
14	ordena	ordenar	to tidy	she tidies	3rd person singular
15	prepara	preparar	to prepare	she prepares	3rd person singular
16	lava	lavar	to wash	she washes	3rd person singular
17	plancha	planchar	to iron	she irons	3rd person singular
18	regresamos	regresar	to return	we return	1st person plural
19	lee	leer	to read	he reads	3rd person singular
20	mira	mirar	to watch	she watches	3rd person singular
21	lee	leer	to read	she reads	3rd person singular
22	canta	cantar	to sing	she sings	3rd person singular
23	cena	cenar	to have dinner	she has dinner	3rd person singular
24	cenar	cenar	to have dinner	infinitive	infinitive
25	estudio	estudiar	to study	I study	1st person singular
26	miran	mirar	to watch	they watch	3rd person plural
27	escuchan	escuchar	to listen	they listen	3rd person plural
28	preparan	preparar	to prepare	they prepare	3rd person plural

My name is Pablo García. We live in Alicante, in Ramón and Cajal Street, number 13. My father works in a bank and my mother works at the school. They work from Monday to Friday.

My father leaves the house at 8 o clock and my mother at 9. My father catches the bus and my mother catches the train.

I study English in the University. I never return to the house at midday, I have lunch in the dining hall of the campus with my classmates. My parents have lunch at work.

My sister doesn´t work until the evening. She tidies the house, prepares the meals, washes the clothes or irons.

We return home at 5 or 6. My father reads the paper, my mother watches the television or reads a book. My sister sings in a bar near to the house and doesn't have dinner with us.

Often, after dinner, I study until 12 at night. My parents watch the television, listen to the radio, or prepare things for the morning.

PRACTICE D:

1. ¿Dónde viven Pablo García y su familia? - Viven en Alicante.
2. ¿Dónde trabajan su madre y padre? - Su padre trabaja en un banco y su madre trabaja en el colegio.
3. ¿Qué días trabajan? - Trabajan de lunes a viernes.
4. ¿A qué hora salen de la casa? - Su padre sale de la casa a las 8 y su madre a las 9.
5. ¿Qué coge su padre? - Su padre coge el autobús.
6. ¿Y su madre? - Su madre coge el tren.
7. ¿Trabaja Pablo? – No. No trabaja.
8. ¿Qué estudia? - Estudia inglés.
9. ¿Dónde estudia? - Estudia en la Universidad.
10. ¿Regresa a casa a mediodía? - Nunca regresa a casa a mediodía.
11. ¿Dónde come? - Come en el comedor del campus con sus compañeros.
12. ¿Dónde comen sus padres? - Sus padres comen en el trabajo.
13. ¿Trabaja su hermana? - Si, su hermana trabaja.
14. ¿Qué hace en la casa? - Ordena la casa, prepara las comidas, lava la ropa o plancha.
15. ¿A qué hora regresan a casa? - Regresan a casa sobre las 5 o 6.
16. ¿Qué hace su madre y padre entonces? - Su padre lee el periodico, y su madre mira la television o lee un libro.
17. ¿Dónde canta su hermana? - Su

hermana canta en un bar cerca de la casa.
18. ¿Cena con ellos? - No, no cena con ellos.
19. ¿Qué hace Pablo despues de cenar? - Muchas veces, después de cenar estudia hasta las doce de la noche.
20. ¿Qué hacen sus padres? - Sus padres miran la tele, escuchan la radio o preparan las cosas para la mañana.

33. DIPHTHONGS - ROOT OR STEM CHANGING VERBS

DIPHTHONGS 1 - PRACTICE A:

1. dormir - to sleep - duermo, duermes, duerme, dormimos, dormís, duermen.
2. costar - to cost - cuesto, cuestas, cuesta, costamos, costáis, cuestan.
3. encontrar - to find/to meet (accidentally) - encuentro, encuentras, encuentra, encontramos, encontráis, encuentran.
4. poder - to "can"/to be able - puedo, puedes, puede, podemos, podéis, pueden.
5. volver - to return - vuelvo, vuelves, vuelve, volvemos, volvéis, vuelven.
6. recordar - to remember - recuerdo, recuerdas, recuerda, recordamos, recordáis, recuerdan.

DIPHTHONGS 1 - PRACTICE B:

1. Duermo muy bien en España.
2. ¿Recuerdas la canción?
3. Vuelven el viernes.
4. Podemos abrir la puerta.
5. Encuentra muchas cosas en su taxi.
6. Los zapatos cuestan 20 euros.

DIPHTHONGS 2 - PRACTICE C:

1. perder - to miss/to lose -
pierdo, pierdes, pierde,
perdemos, perdéis, pierden.
2. comenzar - to commence/to begin -
comienzo, comienzas, comienza,
comenzamos, comenzáis, comienzan.
3. entender – to understand -
entiendo, entiendes,
entiende, entendemos,
entendéis, entienden.
4. preferir – to prefer - prefiero,
prefieres, prefiere, preferimos,
preferís, prefieren.
5. pensar – to think - pienso,
piensas, piensa, pensamos,
pensáis, piensan.
6. querer - to want - quiero,
quieres, quiere, queremos,
queréis, quieren.

DIPHTHONGS 2 - PRACTICE D:

1. La película comienza a las 9.00.
2. No entiendo los verbos españoles.
3. Prefiere vino tinto.
4. Pedro piensa en María cada día/todos los días.
5. Siempre perdemos nuestras gafas de sol.
6. Quieren una casa en Inglaterra y también quieren una casa en España.

DIPHTHONGS 3 - PRACTICE E:

1. conseguir - to get - consigo, consigues, consigue, conseguimos,
conseguís, consiguen.
2. freír - to fry -frío. fríes, fríe, freímos, freís, fríen.
3. pedir - to order/to request/to ask a question - pido, pides, pide,
pedimos, pedís, piden.
4. servir - to order/to be useful for - sirvo, sirves, sirve, servimos,
servís, sirven.
5. medir - to measure - mido, mides, mide, medimos, medís,

miden.
6. seguir - to follow - sigo, sigues, sigue, seguimos, seguís, siguen.

DIPTHONGS 3 - PRACTICE F:

1. Frio hamburguesas los viernes por la noche.
2. Medimos las cortinas.
3. El camarero sirve las bebidas en la terraza.
4. Siempre piden gin y tónica y una cerveza.
5. Conseguimos un trabajo.
6. Sigues el coche amarillo.

34. CONVERSATION PRACTICE DIPHTHONGS

1. ¿Qué normalmente pides en un restaurante chino?
2. ¿A qué hora comienzas a trabajar?
3. ¿Duermes bien en las casas de otra gente/otras personas?
4. ¿Cuánto cuesta una botella de leche en España?
5. ¿Cómo encuentras un buen mecánico en España?
6. ¿A qué hora comienzas a mirar la televisión?
7. ¿Entiendes mucho español?
8. ¿Pierdes muchas cosas en la casa?
9. ¿Prefieres vino tinto, blanco o rosado?
10. ¿A quién recuerdas más del colegio/de la escuela?
11. ¿Vuelves a menudo al Gran Bretaña?
12. ¿Puedes ver el mar de tu casa?
13. ¿Piensas que España es mejor que tu país?
14. ¿Por qué quieres hablar español?
15. ¿Cómo consigues un trabajo bueno en España?
16. ¿Qué normalmente sirven para el desayuno en un restaurante español?
17. Fries mucha comida? (free answer).
18. ¿Sigues este curso? (free answer).

35. DIPHTHONGS - PRACTICE IN CONTEXT

PRACTICE A:

BREAK THE LANGUAGE BARRIER LEVEL 1
vickimariechats@gmail.com

	VERB	INFINITIVE	SPANISH	PERSON
1	is	To be	Ser	3rd person singular
2	lives	To live	Vivir	3rd person singular
3	do not remember	To remember	Recordar (dipthong)	1st person singular
4	I remember	To remember	Recordar (dipthong)	1st person singular
5	is	To be	Estar	3rd person singular
6	he goes	To go	Ir	3rd person singular
7	he orders	To order	Pedir	3rd person singular
8	serves	To serve	Servir	3rd person singular
9	returns	To return	Volver	3rd person singular
10	arrives	To arrive	Llegar	3rd person singular
11	they think	To think	Pensar	3rd person plural
12	they count	To count	Contar	3rd person plural
13	they have	To have	Tener	3rd person plural
14	to buy	To buy	Comprar	Infinitive
15	they want	To want	Querer	3rd person plural
16	costs	To cost	Costar	3rd person singular
17	they have	To have	Tener	3rd person plural
18	they need	To need	Necesitar	3rd person plural
19	they do not sleep	To sleep	Dormir	3rd person plural
20	they think	To think	Pensar	3rd person plural
21	they can	To "can"	Poder	3rd person plural
22	get	To get	Conseguir	Infinitive
23	to buy	To buy	Comprar	Infinitive
24	washes	To wash	Lavar / fregar	3rd person singular
25	starts	To start	Comenzar	3rd person singular
26	to read	To read	Leer	Infinitive
27	they both understand	To understand	Entender	3rd person plural
28	to get	To get	Conseguir	Infinitive
29	they can not	To "can"	Poder	3rd person plural
30	go out	To go out	salir	Infinitive

PRACTICE B:

Pedro Martínez es mecánico y vive en Alicante. No recuerdo exactamente donde, pero recuerdo que su casa está cerca de la playa. Cada/ todos los viernes, va al bar y pide un menú del día que el camarero sirve en la terraza.

Vuelve a su casa después de comer a las 5, y a las 8 llega su novia Carmen. Piensan en su futuro y cuentan el dinero que tienen para comprar una casa. La casa que quieren cuesta 130 mil euros, tienen 100 mil y necesitan más. No duermen por la noche porque piensan en como pueden conseguir bastante dinero para comprar la casa.

Después de cenar, Pedro lava/friega los platos y Carmen comienza a leer el periódico. Los dos comprenden que para conseguir el dinero para la casa no pueden salir por la tarde.

PRACTICE C:

1. ¿Qué hace Pedro? - Pedro es mecánico.
2. ¿Dónde vive? - Vive en Alicante.
3. ¿Recuerdo exactamente donde está su casa? - No, no recuerdas exactamente donde está su casa.
4. ¿Adónde va cada/todos los viernes? - Va al bar cada/todos los viernes.
5. ¿Qué pide? - Pide un menú del día.
6. ¿Dónde sirve el camarero la comida? - El camarero sirve la comida en la terraza.
7. ¿A qué hora vuelve a su casa? - Vuelve a su casa a las 5.
8. ¿A qué hora llega su novia Carmen? - Su novia Carmen llega a las 8.
9. ¿En qué piensan? - Piensan en su futuro.
10. ¿Qué cuentan? - Cuentan el dinero que tienen para comprar una casa.
11. ¿Cuánto cuesta la casa que quieren? - La casa que quieren cuesta 130 mil euros.
12. ¿Cuánto tienen? - Tienen 100 mil.
13. ¿Por qué no pueden dormir por la noche? - No pueden dormir por la noche porque piensan en como pueden conseguir bastante dinero para comprar la casa.
14. ¿Qué hace Pedro después de cenar? - Pedro lava/friega los platos.
15. ¿Qué hace Carmen? - Carmen comienza a leer el periódico.
16. ¿Qué comprenden los dos? - Los dos comprenden que para conseguir el dinero para la casa no pueden salir por la tarde.

36. THE VERB "TENER" – TO HAVE

PRACTICE A:

1. Tengo 10 euros.
2. Tienes mis libros.
3. Tiene un coche nuevo.
4. Tiene las tazas.
5. Tenemos un gato nuevo.
6. Tenéis muchos amigos.
7. Tienen cinco primos.
8. No tengo el dinero.
9. ¿Quién tiene las llaves?
10. ¿Por qué tienes un perro en tu coche?
11. (Ellos) tienen una casa grande en el campo.
12. Tengo mucho cariño por él.
13. ¿Tenéis niños/hijos?
14. No tengo un regalo para su cumpleaños.
15. No tenemos (ningunas) mascotas.

PRACTICE B:

1. Tienes treinta años.
2. María tiene cuarenta y cinco años.
3. Mí coche tiene diez años.
4. ¿Cuántos años tiene tu hermano?
5. Estos chicos tienen quince años.
6. Su gato tiene ocho años.
7. ¿Cuántos años tienen?
8. El pueblo tiene cincuenta años.

PRACTICE C:

1. Porque tengo hambre
2. Porque Juan tiene sed.
3. Porque tienen sueño.
4. Porque tenemos frio.
5. Porque tienes suerte.
6. Porque tienes razón.
7. Porque tenemos prisa.
8. Porque tienen miedo.
9. Porque no tiene razón.
10. Porque tengo calor.

PRACTICE D:

1. Tengo que leer este libro.
2. Tienes que ver esta película.
3. Tenemos que lavar el coche cada sábado.
4. Tiene que abrir la ventana cada mañana.
5. Tenemos que decidir ahora.
6. Tenéis que vender vuestro coche.

7. No tienen que comer el desayuno.
8. Tienes que llevar el perro al parque.
9. Tenemos que comprar vino para la fiesta.
10. No tienes que esperar aquí.

37. "GO-GO" VERBS

PRACTICE A:

1. venir - to come - vengo, vienes, viene, venimos, venís, vienen.
2. decir - to say/to tell - digo, dices, dice, decimos, decís, dicen.
3. hacer - to do/to make - hago, haces, hace, hacemos, hacéis, hacen.
4. oir - to hear - oigo, oyes, oye, oimos, oís, oyen.
5. poner – to put - pongo, pones, pone, ponemos, ponéis, ponen.
6. traer – to bring - traigo, traes, trae, traemos, traéis, traen.

PRACTICE B: (free answers)

1. ¿Sales mucho?
2. ¿Cuántos hermanos tienes?
3. ¿Quién viene a tu casa los domingos?
4. ¿Qué oyes fuera de tu casa por la mañana?
5. ¿Qué dices a un español en su cumpleaños?
6. ¿Qué normalmente pones en tu mesilla de noche?
7. ¿Qué normalmente haces para la comida los domingos?
8. ¿Tienes un perro?
9. ¿Qué dices cuándo estás enfadado?
10. ¿Vienes a España a menudo?
11. ¿Oyes mucho español donde vives?
12. ¿Dónde pones tus llaves en la casa?
13. ¿Cuándo haces una paella?
14. ¿Qué ropa/ropas traes contigo cuando vienes a España?

38. "GUSTAR" – TO LIKE/PLEASE

PRACTICE A:

1. Les gusta nadar.
2. ¿Te gusta el chocolate?
3. Nos gustan los coches rápidos.
4. ¿Os gusta leer?

5. Le gusta nadar.
6. Me gusta cantar.
7. Nos gusta salir los sábados.
8. Le gusta salir con los/sus amigos.
9. ¿Te gusta estudiar español?
10. Les gusta la comida española.
11. Me gustan los gatos.
12. No me gustan los perros.
13. ¿No te gusta el fútbol?
14. No nos gusta viajar en/por avión.
15. Me gustan estos zapatos.

39. "IR" - TO GO - THE HIGHLY IRREGULAR 'IR' VERB

PRACTICE A:

1. ¿Adónde vas?
2. Van a la playa todas las semanas.
3. Vamos al bar cada domingo.
4. ¿Adónde vas los sábados?
5. Va al trabajo en el autobús.
6. Voy al hospital cada martes por la mañana.
7. Cuando necesito verduras, voy al mercadillo.
8. Mi hermano siempre va al futból.
9. Para conseguir un permiso, tenéis que ir al Ayuntamiento.
10. ¿Cuándo van al cine?
11. Voy a España cada año.
12. Vamos a su casa los lunes.
13. Van a su casa los martes.
14. ¿Vas mucho a las tiendas?
15. ¿Por qué no vas a su casa?

40. TIA CARMEN- AUNT CARMEN

PRACTICE A:

VERB IN CONTEXT	INFINITIVE	SPANISH	PERSON
1. is	To be	ser	3 p sing
2. lives	To live	vivir	3 p sing
3. lives	To live	vivir	3 p sing
4. lives	To live	vivir	3 p sing
5. has	To have	tener	3 p sing
6. is	To be	ser	3 p sing

BREAK THE LANGUAGE BARRIER LEVEL 1
vickimariechats@gmail.com

7. is	To be	ser	3 p sing
8. has	To have	tener	3 p sing
9. is	To be	ser	3 p sing
10. is	To (have-age)	ser	3 p sing
11. is	To be	ser	3 p sing
12. has	To have	tener	3 p sing
13. is	To be	ser	3 p sing
14. has	To have	tener	3 p sing
15. finishes	To finish	terminar	3 p sing
16. arrives	To arrive	llegar	3 p sing
17. is	To be	estar	3 p sing
18. goes up	To go up	subir	3 p sing
19. she doesn't like	To like (please)	gustar	3 p plural
20. wants	To want	querer	3 p sing
21. to do	To do	hacer	infinitive
22. arrives	To arrive	llegar	3 p sing
23. takes out	To take out	sacar	3 p sing
24. opens	To open	abrir	3 p sing
25. enters	To enter	entrar	3 p sing
26. comes	To come	veniir	3 p sing
27. to say	To say	decir	infinitive
28. makes	To make	hacer	3 p sing
29. enters	To enter	entrar	3 p sing
30. turns on	To turn on	encender	3 p sing
31. goes into	To go in	entrar en	3 p sing
32. makes	To make	hacer	3 p sing
33. returns	To return	volver	3 p sing
34. reads	To read	leer	3 p sing
35. she sits down	To sit down	sentarse	3 p sing
36. starts	To start	empezar/comenzar	3 p sing
37. to answer	To answer	contestar	infinitive
38. she switches off	To switch off	apagar	3 p sing
39. goes to	To go to	ir a	3 p sing
40. she prepares	To prepare	preparar	3 p sing
41. turns on	To turn on	encender	3 p sing
42. calls	To call	llamar	3 p sing
43. they chat	To chat	charlar	3 p plural
44. washes	To wash	lavar	3 p sing
45. decides	To decide	decidir	3 p sing
46. to go to bed	To go to bed	acostarse/ ir a la cama	infinitive

PRACTICE B:

Carmen Pérez es mi tia, hermana de mi madre. Vive en Murcia en el sur de España. Vive en un piso/apartamento pequeño, limpio y ordenado en el centro de la ciudad. Vive sola pero tiene una gata pequeña y blanca. El nombre de la gata es Luna. Carmen es alta, morena, y tiene ojos grises. Es muy guapa y tiene treinta y cinco años. Es/ está soltera pero tiene un novio, Luis.

Tía Carmen es abogada y tiene una oficina grande cerca su casa. Termina el trabajo a las siete de la tarde y cuando llega a casa está muy cansada. En su piso/ apartamento hay dos dormitorios, un cuarto de baño, un salón, un comedor, un despacho y una cocina.

Sube las escaleras como no le gustan los ascensores y quiere hacer más ejercicio. Cuando llega a la tercera planta saca su llave, abre la puerta y entra. Luna siempre viene para decir "hola". Hace mucho ruido para una gata.

Carmen entra en el despacho y enciende el ordenador. Entonces entra en la cocina donde hace un café. Vuelve/regresa al despacho y lee sus correos electrónicos. Se sienta y empieza a contestarlos.

Después apaga el ordenador y va a la cocina donde prepara la cena, entonces enciende la tele en el salón. Su novio Luis a menudo la llama por teléfono. Charlan un rato corto, y después Carmen lava los platos y decide acostarse/ ir a la cama.

PRACTICE C:

1. ¿Dónde vive Carmen Pérez? Vive en Murcia en el sur de España.
2. ¿Cómo es su piso/ apartamento y dónde está?
3. ¿Con quién vive? Vive con su gata.
4. ¿Cuánto años tiene? Tiene treinta y cinco años.
5. ¿Está casada? No, es/ está soltera.
6. ¿Qué hace y dónde trabaja? Es abogada y trabaja en una oficina cerca de su casa.
7. ¿A qué hora termina el trabajo? Termina el trabajo a las siete.
8. ¿Cómo está cuándo llega a casa? Está muy cansada.
9. ¿Qué hay en su apartamento/ piso? Hay dos dormitorios, un baño, un salón, un

comedor, un despacho, y una cocina.
10. ¿Por qué sube las escaleras? Porque no le gustan los ascensores y quiere hacer más ejercicio.
11. ¿Qué hace cuando llega a la tercera planta? Saca su llave, abre la puerta y entra.
12. ¿Quién viene para decir "hola"? Su gata Luna.
13. ¿Qué hace en el despacho? Enciende el ordenador.
14. ¿Qué hace en la cocina? Hace un café.
15. ¿Dónde lee sus correos electrónicos? En el despacho.
16. ¿Qué hace después de contestarlos? Apaga el ordenador y va a la cocina donde prepara la cena.
17. ¿Quién la llama a menudo por teléfono? Su novio Luis.
18. ¿Qué hace Carmen después de lavar los platos? Decide acostarse/ ir a la cama.

www.ingramcontent.com/pod-product-compliance
Lightning Source LLC
Chambersburg PA
CBHW081944070426
42450CB00015BA/3330